Curflexion
Living the Infinite Space of Being

Dr. Pedro Cortina

INQUOS Publications
Vancouver, Canada

INQUOS Publications
Vancouver, B.C
www.inquos.com

ISBN 1511837969
ISBN13 978-1511837965

Important Notice to Reader

All content and practices in this book are presented as an invitation into the exploration of our internal world for the purposes of self-discovery and personal inquiry.

If readers choose to engage with the content and practices presented in this book, they do so under their own responsibility. The content and practices in this book are not intended or presented to advice, counsel, treat, diagnose, prescribe, or cure any condition, or address any specific situation.

Individuals naturally remain wholly responsible for their own understanding, experience and actions, and should seek appropriately qualified, licensed or professional support to address their particular needs.

For all who seek
boundless inner
freedom

www.curflexion.com

Origins

I was visited by death early on in my life. When I was 6 years old, our car was hit head on by a passenger bus while my mother was driving from the cabin to the city after a weekend of sun, water, and fun. The impact killed her instantly along with my very young 2 year old brother. I survived the crash but at that point, my life changed considerably.

As sometimes happens when you are presented with deep and intense experiences at a young age, my perception of life would now include a profound need to make sense of existence. My philosophical drive was certainly more intense than that of the average person would at my age; and my need for understanding was simply unquenchable. My mind was inundated early on with deep existential questions and concerns, as well as with a profound need to figure out things at the *designer* level.

By the age of 10, I would be easily and deeply transported to blissful worlds through standard religious practice. Contemplation would seem to come to me naturally. As early as 16, I was reading profound philosophical texts and practicing several meditation techniques. I was also finding my tribe. I found the love and companionship, as well as the kinship and connection of those with whom I would share extraordinary experiences in the coming decades that I could've never imagined possible at the time.

During my early 20s, I would engage in serious explorations of the exciting realms of Shamanic traditions. I would also become fully absorbed in the study and active practice of Tibetan Tantra. I further became intensely immersed in the Mahamudra, Dzogchen, and Advaita traditions of non-dual philosophy.

I finished a degree in Western Philosophy from an exemplary Jesuit University and devoted my life to education. I further finished masters and doctoral degrees in education, specializing in consciousness-based education and educational leadership from the University of British Columbia and the University of Calgary.

One particular afternoon, as I sat with friends, I suddenly began to feel the signs of what would become an intense panic attack. My pulse raided my body, I broke out in an intense cold sweat and my breath became extremely shallow. I clenched my hands together in an attempt to anchor myself. My heart felt as if it was going to explode. There was a form of silence in the background that appeared to be the most inhospitable element in the universe.

After what seemed to have been an infinity, on that particular afternoon *I gave up completely*. From the depths of my being, and with every cell of my body, *I let go entirely*. I released everything in an instant, utterly handing myself over to complete internal annihilation. I had nothing to sustain, no one to be, nothing to defend, nothing to fix, no one to save and in that moment, what remained of my illusory self completely dissolved.

Still in that room, I suddenly experienced that I was somehow *staring directly at myself from myself,* with no form, no distractions, no thoughts, no wants, no needs, no expectations, and no hope clouding this direct and extraordinary experience. I was living a form of *profound self-recognition* of the infinite and indescribable space that supports everything. An exquisite, boundless, and completely held state of Being that needs absolutely nothing on our part to be sustained.

In the following months, I began to incessantly write poetry in an attempt to describe this space of *self-reflection as reflection.* After a while, the poetry stopped and was followed by several more months of writing prose, thus giving birth to a 250-page manuscript that was the first rough draft of the book you hold in your hands now. As I shared the manuscript with my friends, family, and colleagues, I received brilliant feedback and suggestions that would make the original manuscript more readable and accessible to others. I have also looked to relate this content to the work of other authors in the fields of applied philosophy, neuroscience and counselling, in an attempt to give it some additional context.

This book is the result of more than twenty years of personal exploration crowned by an unexpected and extraordinary discovery:

Immediately behind our human experience of internal separation and suffering, there is a vast and open space of understanding, connection and compassion, where we become fully alive and at peace with existence and with ourselves.

~ We can get there ~

My most humble and profound appreciation goes to those who keep the *Infinite Space of Being* accessible to all who seek its exquisite embrace. With their inspiration, practices, guidance, and texts, we are able to rekindle the lamp that guides us through the path of confusion.

Tania, Sebastian, Julian, Paige, Adrian, Keith, Robert, Valerie, Karen, and Ryan, your feedback and suggestions for this manuscript have been invaluable. Thank you!

Curflexion

Introduction

Let's open the door to the infinite!
Let's allow ourselves undefined!

Without center,
without Self,
without
expectation.

Curving into our same reflection,
nothing remains obscure.

In perfect openness of endless space,
we embody everything!

What is Curflexion? When we step between opposing mirrors we are stepping into an infinite reflection. Imagine now that your body becomes transparent while you are standing between those two mirrors. What would you see? You would see pure, endless space. You would be looking at infinity from infinity and hence subject and object would disappear, eliminating all source of conflict, allowing for perfect space, wholesome spontaneity, inner sustainability, and profound fulfillment to manifest. *I call this state Curflexion.*

In Curflexion, there is no grasping, no sense of being incomplete; therefore, we experience Being at its fullest. An answer to our suffering condition as human beings actually lies in allowing for the pristine, endless space of Curflexion to manifest, rather than attempting to fix our problems by juxtaposing positivity with negativity or trying to find lasting refuge from suffering in the many alternatives we are usually offered.

The way to access Curflexion is not through a particular method, strategy, sequential procedure or mechanism. The fact is that there is actually nothing to change or oppose. In essence, we access Curflexion naturally and effortlessly as a result of allowing the profound assimilation and deep experiential understanding of the true nature of our internal reality.

The great majority of times in our daily lives, our consciousness-as-mirror is not reflecting another mirror, but rather an endless stream of objects, situations, thoughts, emotions, evaluations, judgments, hopes, fears, wants, needs, expectations, and plans. For some reason, there seems to be an innate impulse coming from somewhere within ourselves that hopes to interact with all these manifesting forms, with the wish to solidify our experience of these same objects and situations; as well as of ourselves. As a result, it happens that we forget that we are simply a clean, spotless mirror and we get caught up with the forms being reflected in the mirror, thereby giving birth to one of the most confusing and burdensome aspects of existence. We commonly refer to this aspect of existence simply as *suffering*, but it comes with a myriad of other names and forms of manifestation that include tension, confusion, anxiety, stress, worry, dread and many, many others that we tend to experience on a daily basis. Each of us has our own particular concoction of this brew and we seem to identify suffering in uniquely different ways, battling uniquely different situations, forces, conditions and challenges.

When we eliminate subject and object, as is the case in Curflexion, suffering vanishes because there is no evaluator. Hence we eliminate the source of suffering. There is no comparison, no expectation, no separation and no strife. The notions of *you* and *me, yours and mine* take the back seat to the understanding of *is*.

Most of humanity's self improvement methods are based on a "fix it" model (Hayes 2005), in other words, these methods are based on an *oppositional model* in which we attempt to oppose or resist negative thoughts or experiences with positive thoughts or experiences in order to fix the negative thoughts or experiences. Most transformational strategies, such as evaluating, conditioning, striving, visualizing, hoping, attracting, and accumulating, are generally at the core of these methods – from finding the secret recipe to everlasting wealth and health to engaging in some form of cumulative practice to achieve full clarity or spiritual realization. In the great and vast majority of cases, the end result of applying these oppositional approaches, after much practice, dedication, investment, and commitment, is far from what we expected and tends to involve some form of disillusionment or failure.

In this book, we will explore each of the composites of human experience that keep us being part of our apparently endless, exhausting, confusing and painful separation condition, in order to understand and alleviate our situation. We will also explore a practical model to embody Curflexion so that we may finally step into the vast open space of freedom that we intuitively know exists beyond our daily experience of confusion, separation, anxiety and overall suffering.

This book is certainly not to be presented as an academic or even necessarily as a structurally logical approximation to address a gradual understanding and systematization of the elimination of suffering. Far from being a psychological manual or a traditional self-help book, this work is intended to be *an engaging and applied philosophical and educational invitation* towards experiencing the fully independent, self-sustaining, self-fulfilling and entirely self-contained state of Curflexion.

All content and practices in this book are presented as an invitation into the exploration of our internal world for the purposes of self-discovery and personal inquiry. This book is not intended to advice, counsel, treat, diagnose, prescribe, or cure any condition or address any specific situation. Any one who chooses to engage with the content and practices presented in this book, will be doing so under their own responsibility and will naturally remain wholly responsible for their own understanding, experience and actions. It is important to remind ourselves that when needed, we should seek appropriately qualified, licensed or professional support to address our particular needs.

We will face some interesting challenges throughout this book. *Curflexion is an existential phenomenon that appears beyond conceptualization and language.* Language is indeed our best form of communication thus far; nevertheless, language in all its complexity, will often appear to frame our exploration and experience of Curflexion in what may appear to be limited or contradictory terms. I would like to invite you to allow yourself to find and embody the experience of Curflexion beyond language, beyond conceptualization and beyond the apparent contradictions we will certainly be facing throughout this book.

This manuscript will not offer us a traditional presentation of concepts to be defined or constructed sequentially or even logically at times. The principles that will be presented in this book may further appear to be counter intuitive and therefore, their understanding and implementation may require a different approximation than what we are generally used to when reading a book. In some cases, this may imply reviewing paragraphs, pages, or sections a few times in order to fully allow for the essence of what is being presented to come through.

In the early chapters, ideas and concepts that may initially seem unclear will become self evident as we address themes or practices in the later sections of the book. In some cases, a second or third reading might become considerably more rewarding than the first one. It may also be useful for some people to reread the entire book from time to time, a few months apart, in order to retrace the path into the endless space of unabridged inner freedom.

The main ideas presented in this book will be reiterated throughout on several occasions. The idea here is not to be simply repetitive, but rather, given that the content will tend to be naturally counter intuitive at times, to serve the reader with a constant reminder of the most important ideas in the book, while addressing new themes in subsequent sections.

This book has been written with the intention of offering a profoundly transformative tool for those who are deeply tired of the distractions and self perpetuating cycles of dissatisfaction that we tend to experience as human beings. It is a vehicle for those who are ready to find meaning and clarity in a profound, non-oppositional and non-dual approximation to ultimate inner freedom.

The way to embody Curflexion is not through a particular methodology or a strategy; it is not through a sequential procedure or mechanism. We achieve Curflexion naturally and effortlessly as a result of the profound assimilation and understanding of the nature of our internal reality. For some reason or another, as human beings, we seem to experience several intriguing misconceptions as to how our internal world actually works, often binding us into a continual experience of dissatisfaction and expectation of some future situation that will be better than now, or trying to fix a past experience that is now certainly unavailable.

This book will guide us through an exploration of our complex human condition by clarifying three main paradoxes that, when profoundly assimilated, will redress the nature of our inherent confusion whilst also showing us how to completely eliminate it. The profound experiential understanding of these three paradoxes will result in the natural resolution of the basic misunderstandings concerning the nature of our internal condition.

The result of this realignment generally produces a profound relaxation in our need to conceptualize, fix, structure, solidify and control our surroundings; to the point where we end up opening and accessing the space of all possibilities, a space where there is no lack, no effort, no tension, no doubt and which offers a complete grounding, full clarity, willingness and understanding of our human experience. This approach is not based on any particular philosophical or ideological understanding or an inaccessible set of assumptions, it is absolutely open to all individuals, regardless of their background, previous experience or prevailing beliefs.

This book has been divided into seven sections. The first section will present the basic problem of our general human situation: the fact that we suffer, how we suffer, and why we suffer. In this section, suffering is explored as a foundation to our ultimate liberation from this condition.

The second section will present three paradoxical misunderstandings that will allow for the profound clarification of our human condition in order to experientially allow for Being to fully manifest. The profound experiential embodiment of these paradoxes opens the door for lasting personal transformation and a clear path into Curflexion.

The third section will present a process of deconstruction and realignment that will question and reframe some of the most basic and profound concepts we have assimilated in life as now seen through the lens of the three paradoxes. Some of these concepts include dissolution, depression, death, free will, relationships, and purpose.

The fourth section will present a re-evaluation of our overall possibilities given our new understanding and application of the three paradoxes as experienced through our full embodiment and sustainment of Being. In this section, we will explore themes such as oneness, accountability, responsibility, compassion, surrender, and willingness.

Finally, sections five, six, and seven will introduce, present and substantiate a series of concrete, non-oppositional explorations or practices to support the process of understanding, thus allowing attainment of Curflexion.

May this book find its way precisely to where its practical understanding and application may result in profound personal transformation.

1

The Problem

O scoundrels and impostors of the night,
you seem to be the masters of this shed.
You boast of holding the key to tomorrow
unlocking the coffins of the fore.

I stare at you in complete exhaustion,
pinned to the wall of high and low.
May I take one more breath?
May I explore one more answer?
May I seek another refuge?

O scoundrels and impostors of the night,
I have been yours for far too long.
And here I rest,
trapped,
forgotten,
lost.

Suffering

Suffering is so common to human experience that we are used to simply accounting for it as a given, while we try to continue with life as best we can: In some cases, trying not to think too much about the cause of our suffering and in other cases completely consumed by it. We often appear to devise structures, rules and standards in an attempt to control suffering without much success (Hayes, 2005). Many social and organizational structures manifest as a response to our suffering condition and are mostly designed, developed and managed with suffering as the main frame of reference.

When we are able to observe our internal human experience, we can see that as basic mental images arise in our consciousness, we instinctively tend to identify, label, separate, categorize and concretize their content into broad positive or negative categories. We additionally tend to categorize these initial dualizations into a further endless stream of additional divisive subtleties. These subtleties generate an internal positioning that usually causes us to settle into one of two possible camps: the one we want or the one we do not want. Regardless of what these may look like, these two possible existential dualities immediately and automatically generate internal tension; a kind of basic *positional tension,* as we seek to attract and keep what we naturally consider pleasurable and defend ourselves from what we would naturally consider painful.

In addition, it would be easy to ascertain that at times, mental images, thoughts and emotions are entirely random and nonsensical - from crazy and strange to innocent and irrational. It appears as if we were constantly being called upon to make sense, to react to or do something about our internal experience. So, if our thoughts and emotional processes appear to be random or unstable at times, then they will provide limited reliability and consistency for working on them or interacting with them, again generating a form of basic *instability tension.* Given this situation, our resulting strategy is to tend to identify, align and support the thoughts that apparently provide or support who we think we are. At the same time, trying to discard, eliminate or battle with the thoughts that reflect who we do not think we are or who we think we should not be or even simply, thoughts that somehow imply inner inconsistency or dissonance.

This is followed by important realization when it comes to noticing our thoughts and emotions. This is the fact that there is absolutely no way of permanently controlling our thoughts and emotions. We may be able to induce a certain level of influence that may last for a while, only to succumb to a negative aspect of that same influence later on (Hayes, 2005). It may be that we become disillusioned with something or even with our own expectation to maintain a positive inner environment. Thoughts are also often random or misleading and they do not inherently support or validate our own self perception. In many cases, thoughts and emotions simply manifest independently of our hopes or expectations. Consequently, thoughts and emotions demand attention, allegiance, resistance and some form of internal action when they appear as problematic or inconsistent with who we believe we are or should be.

We also seem to experience *existential tension*. This kind of tension is generally a more profound experience. It deals with the big questions of life and tends to demand we take life considerably more personally and seriously than may be needed, questioning such things as: our relationship with reality and the way things are at a designer level; why two eyes and not four; why wings only on a few species; why do we suffer; why do people hate; why the atrocities in this world; why crime; why suicide; is the world inherently bad; are humans inherently good? When it comes to existential tension, we also may see ourselves addressing complications that revolve around our purpose in life, our passion, the direction we want to grow in, as well as countless other possibilities regarding social expectations such as the notions of punishment, religion, morality, right action and transcendence, amongst others.

Socially, we set up expectations for particular individuals or groups. This kind of *conditioning tension* could be family or community driven; it can happen in smaller groups or in large social settings. Conditioning generates tension because of the basic fact that there is dissonance between what the individual may consider in her or his best interest and what the group (be it large or small) may consider to be in the best interest of the individual or the group. Here, tension manifests as the gap between personal expectations and group expectations.

We also seem to experience *instability tension* when it comes to making long-term choices. Let us see if this sounds familiar. One day we appear to love our job and the next day we seem to hate it. One day we appear to love our family and another day we would be happily to patch them up to better suit our needs. We sometimes suffer because we have something and then we suffer because we lack the exact same thing. We seem to sometimes curse, disparage and eliminate something, only then to cry for its loss. It would appear as if our will does not have an ultimate, secure spot or settling platform from where we can feel sustained, content and satisfied. We seem to be immersed in a constant, often contradictory and at times overwhelmingly cyclical burden of wants and rejections.

We are also socialized to do our best to achieve love, career, companionship, independence, and success.

Yet, after consistently striving to achieve these goals for many years, every one of these experiences clearly ends up producing or having to deal with some form of *positional* or *instability* tension through some form of consequential, pre-existing, or concurrent negative effect or experience. In other words, *while we strive towards attainment, we suffer the lack of attainment; while we achieve a form of attainment, we suffer the lack of speed of attainment; and while we attain, we suffer the lack of security and continuity in attainment.* This seems to be a continuing cycle that self-perpetuates based on the expectation of a positive future permanent attainment.

It would be easy to see that given this situation, we may easily become seekers and willing clients of some form of magical solution. We may want to find the secret of that unique and perfect experience or element that would seem to be missing and that would actually allow us to permanently achieve our ultimate goal or expectation or at least one or some of them. As a result, we end up going around in circles, hoping that each time we come around, we find the way out of the cycle in a positive and permanent way.

No matter what our life looks like, we tend to have some kind of sincere and profound existential complaint. It can be about love, it can be about loneliness, it can be about wealth, it can be about poverty, it can be about mediocrity, it can be about common sense, it can be about loss, it can be about gain, it can be about hurt, it can be about liberation, it can be about joy or it can even be about happiness.

Therefore, we can safely conclude that tension and suffering are a generalized human condition (Hayes, 2005) from light unease to tremendous heaviness, anxiety, confusion, depression or tragedy. Forms and intensity vary, but the dualisms of suffering and joy, contraction and expansion, rejection and wanting are consistent and can certainly be counted upon. This does not mean that life should be discarded entirely as a dreadful and unbearable experience, however it does mean that tension and suffering certainly account for a considerable portion of the experience of the majority of human beings, with some taking on a larger load than others.

The wonderful news at this point is that *there is a way out of this situation.* That this condition stems from a genuine, innocent and profound misunderstanding about how our internal world works and how we should relate to some of the most basic elements of our human experience. In the latter sections of this book, we will explore several ways to internalize this understanding to the point where it allows for a natural immersion into the pristine and direct experience of Curflexion.

Innocence

Why so much suffering? What is its origin? Why so much confusion? Who are we to hold accountable or blame for all this? What produces this seemingly endless cycle that appears to lure us like moths to the candlelight? Interestingly enough, as human beings, in our need to identify who or what should be responsible for our condition, we generally tend to assign responsibility for our suffering to someone or something. In knowing who or what is responsible, we would then be able to demand its cessation. From here, a great list of possible culprits arises that enumerates all kinds of parties potentially guilty of our suffering condition, from individuals, cultures, family, or society, all the way to our closest or dearest relationships or even ourselves.

So, who are we to blame about this prevailing condition of constant dissatisfaction and confusion? *Actually, no one.* As difficult as this may seem to our learned sense of justice and retribution, in this case, absolutely no one is responsible and no one is to blame. We are all innocent in our confusion, in our suffering and in our apparently bad choices.

Distraction is truly pervasive in our world, and distraction is one of our most common responses to internal confusion, dissonance or incongruence. When we see confusion in this world, we may generally prefer to distract ourselves instead of allowing understanding, confusion, or pain to be felt. We generally fail to open up to understand the conditions that led to those circumstances and why our hopeful oppositional countermeasures continue to fail. We naturally tend not to get close to pain and we also tend to resist most forms of its manifestation.

As we are innocent of this condition, we are, interestingly enough, also innocently supporting this suffering situation at the same time. In other words, we are innocently feeding this condition, as if trapped in a dream of constant distraction, and entirely missing the true point of what is happening and the actual situation that is sustaining our confusion. We seem to be trapped in an apparently endless cycle of attainment and loss that is far from stable and that consistently seems to demand our internal engagement and allegiance to one side of the cycle in order to tentatively appease the frequency and intensity of the dualizations we seem to consistently experience.

We are honestly confused because we believe that our internal world should work in the same way that the external world works and that we should oppose what seems to be the source of our problems (Hayes, 2005). When something goes wrong in our external environment, we tend to diagnose the situation, identify a solution for it, buy into the solution and fix the problem by establishing or implementing the solution to achieve the result we want. Easy. Internally, when it comes to human beings, our experience does not work in the same way as it does externally and here lies a paradox that disallows human beings from experiencing the same efficiency they experience externally when it comes to dealing with our internal realm and, therefore, when dealing with personal suffering.

To move ahead in our exploration, it is very important to look into what we are referring to when we say "I", "me", or "myself". This will help us understand the intricacies of suffering as well as the potential cessation of suffering. To explore this condition, we will need to take a closer look into the phenomenon of *self* as one of the most intriguing manifestations of our human condition and one that requires close examination in order for us to understand how suffering is created and begin to clarify how suffering can entirely be resolved.

Who Are We
Talking To?

Let us take a moment to look into one of our most basic and common human experiences. From the moment we awake to the moment we fall asleep (and also while we dream actually), we seem to be engaged in some form of continual internal conversation. Interestingly enough, instead of finding this incredibly odd, we seem to resolve this apparent situation by assuming that first of all, this experience is entirely normal, common and natural, and furthermore, that we are simply having a form of internal dialogue with ourselves. We usually leave it at that.

This experience is so common that most of the time we do not seem to consider this dialogue to be too important and sometimes we are not able to even notice its effects on ourselves, let alone on others. We are generally also unable to experience its subtle comings and goings as well as its profound intricacies and implications. Everybody seems to experience this phenomenon. It is also quite interesting to notice that this condition is as ubiquitous to human beings as suffering itself and may very well be one of the most basic phenomena defining what we understand to be the human experience.

All previous things considered, when we actually take the time to look deeply into this constant internal conversation with ourselves, we are plunged into a vast and at times, inexplicable experience. We are presented with an endless stream of thoughts, concepts, assumptions and reactions along with a constantly elusive sense of grounding or origin to these. We are presented with a conversation or rather several conversations, that are full of possibilities, evaluations, considerations, fears, projections, hopes and expectations. We are presented with the need to manage, upkeep, and maintain these conversations in a way that sustains our internal world according to the standards and expectations that we have set up for ourselves through a profoundly complex system of consensual socialization. Additionally, while we do this, we are also hoping to solidify a sustainable and reliable experience of who we think we are.

The first problem we may encounter is the fact that we would certainly seem to be having a conversation with what appears to be someone entirely different or someone who is not the initial voice. When we notice that a thought suddenly appears or an emotion suddenly manifests naturally and effortlessly, we tend to engage this thought or emotion by starting an internal process in which we seem to act as if we were actually speaking to someone else. For example, if we notice that a feeling of sadness appears suddenly, we may internally ask, "Why am I feeling sad?" Then comes an answer that may say, for example, "Oh, because I didn't get the job." To which you again could reply, "I'm sure they already had an internal candidate." You, again, may counter reply, "Well, maybe I was just not good enough" and on and on in a seemingly endless process that interacts, addresses, ponders, evaluates and dissects what is being presented in our consciousness-as-mirror. This is a form of continuous dialogical narration supported by thoughts, feelings and emotions that generally never stops as long as we are conscious.

So, who are we actually talking to? Again, we sincerely think we are taking to ourselves. Who else is there to talk to, right? We also tend to believe and argue that in this self-dialogue, we are making sense of our world, its complications and ourselves. Yet, there may be something else going on. Indeed, we are not talking to someone else, in particular, because there is no one else there and at the same time, we are not talking to ourselves either because there seems to be no central origin to the conversation.

If we examine this process in detail, we may notice that we seem to be talking to and from *several frames of reference that tend to act independently from each other and that are very far from a stable, consistent and unified self.* In

27

other words, we seem to experience a series of conversations with and from several different internal perspectives, which are mutually exclusive sometimes, and others inclusive from one another. It is as if we have accumulated several distinctly different mind models or mind structures through our social learning, conditioning and human interaction that end up constituting competing, self sustaining and self validating internal frameworks of their own (Hood, 2012).

This is a form of cyclical process, in which we appear to be trying to make sense of our internal experience, of our thoughts and emotions. We are trying to control, make sense of or manage this process as much as we can. We seem to be seeking to identify some form of internal, consistent and solid grounding, in which we could fundamentally base our experience or internal narrative. We are building an illusory self (Hood, 2012) and therefore, we are building a narrative about who we imagine ourselves to be.

Unfortunately, in the end, this effort and methodology towards validation and sustainment of internal solid grounding seems to be rarely successful, given that we are clearly constantly changing our perspective, preferences, points of view, levels of satisfaction, dissatisfaction as well as our overall levels of suffering and happiness as we have previously seen.

In summary, what seems to be a simple internal dialogue also appears to be a universal human phenomenon that generates considerable maintenance, confusion and complication in our ability to experience life with clarity, containment and peace; that is, our ability to experience a stable, consistent, and congruent internal experience of self. In the following sections, we will explore this phenomenon and its implications in the development and experience of what we may perceive to be our illusory self – that apparent center of our internal experience that we refer to as who we are.

Self-Illusion

Let us explore then who we think we are and what is this apparent unifying experience we call "me", "myself", or "I". As I was saying before, we seem to constantly be having an ongoing internal conversation with ourselves. Further more interesting questions would be: Who or what is *listening* to this conversation? Who have I been talking to and who has apparently been listening and maybe even deciding my life for me all along? Who am I? What part of me is me? Why am I sometimes completely sure about myself and sometimes I feel so lost? Why do I sometimes feel that I am clear of what I want and sometimes I feel entirely confused? Why do I make choices that I later regret? Why is it so difficult to find my passion and direction in life? What is this apparently central, sustained and integral experience of I?

These questions are particularly important because in them lies the true potential to understand who we really are as well as the root of our mysterious suffering condition and the potential liberation of this same condition. These are indeed important questions to ask ourselves, but for one reason or another, we seem to have learned to generally ignore or disregard this profound line of inquiry and incorporate our internal dialogue into our usually noisy external experience, which is naturally assumed to be part of our everyday life.

Our internal dialogue tends to become unnoticed in the same way we experience the radio when driving, when we incorporate the words or music into our routine to the point where these are apparently not even there anymore. Although we think we do not notice these distractions, later on, we find ourselves singing the song that was playing on the radio. Hence, it is important to see that even if apparently unnoticed, these internal narratives still seem to have considerable influence and a clear effect on our everyday experience. Overall, this underlying noise may be the source of much confusion and distraction, which in the end results in strengthening a cycle of internal instability, doubt, projection and tension that leads to our human condition of separation.

On the other hand, when we consciously notice the internal discourse and we pay attention to it, we seem to come to the firm and profoundly erroneous belief that this internal discourse is the central experience of who we really are; *that some form of normalization or average of our usually random, at times contradictory and often unstable in-*

ner experience is what we consider to be our true self (Hood, 2012). This internal experience would be similar to having different identities inside of us that are constantly interacting, hoping to interpret our life situation in a way that solidifies the experience of who we think we might be.

We could use the analogy of ourselves as a vessel where several independent skippers are trying to take control of the helm wheel using various strategies to validate, justify or argue why each of them should be running the show. For them, the trick is how to convince and solidify leadership above the different voices and impulses (other skippers) by amassing as much internal validation and outside confirmation as possible. In other words, while attempting to position themselves as the unquestionable foundational axiom of who we are or as the original reference point for what we want or what we are all about. This is how the experience of a *central illusory self* is created and sustained. Our experience of a central, unified self is, therefore, simply an internal creation that is built through a perceptional average of stimuli that we amalgamate together in order to experience a cohesive experience of life (Hood, 2012).

Basic consciousness acts like a simple mirror that reflects whatever appears in front of it, regardless of it being material or immaterial. We seem to be conscious of thoughts, emotions, language, ideas, feelings, dreams, imaginings and intuitions, as well as all kinds of elements and situations of the physical world around us that manifest in endless forms, combinations and derivatives of these combinations. Everything we can conceive of or perceive – be it internal or external – is perceived through consciousness. Consciousness acts like a simple mirror of what manifests in reference to our overall perception. This mirror-like phenomenon is the most basic component of who we are.

Following *consciousness-as-mirror*, we find a first layer of perceptional activity, which can be called *Neutral Form*. As stated above form does not necessarily imply only material form, but it would include all other manifestations of perceived form. All the same, at this level, all form perceived is simply *devoid* of any evaluation, interpretation, rationalization, dualization, categorization, conceptualization, projection or judgment. Thoughts, emotions and sensations as well as our perception of objects, nature, trees, pots and pans exist simply as is and prior to all possible judgment, differentiation, or interpretation.

A second layer that we can call *Structural Interpretation* then generally influences anything and everything that appears on the layer of Neutral Form. In this layer, we seem to evaluate, interpret, compare, judge, analyze, dualize and synthesize Neutral Form and, hence, establish a relationship with form that creates expectations of either rejection or attachment to and from endless constructs of our own creation. This constructive and interpretative process is based on social conditioning, random thoughts and emotions, but more importantly, personal ideas and projections based on past memories, past joys or an imagined future.

This process is somewhat unreliable as well as clearly unstable and arbitrary.

In other words, at the level of Structural Interpretation, *we appear to create an almost entirely imaginary world that only touches reality in very few and limited points.* Even when it does, it does so with the complication of needing to interact, interpret and express this experience through the constructed and limited conceptual structure we call language. In doing so, we force our experience into a dualistic pondering of polarized perceptions and interpretations of neutral phenomena, *reducing our full experience of Being to a limited dualistic abstraction, conceptualization and rationalization that is far removed from Being's full expression and potential.*

Interestingly enough, this layer of Structural Interpretation is the layer where all the skippers live and where they are all trying their best to each take control of the helm wheel. They are the internalization and combination of countless voices that have influenced us so far, such as parents, sons, daughters, siblings, bosses, lovers, as well as their endless possible combinations, derivations, amalgamations and ramifications and, therefore, many other influences that we misguidedly internally believe to be ourselves. These apparent identities are constantly making assessments, evaluating risk, amassing evidence and trying to justify and solidify their existence as best they can in order to take control and successfully reify our own existence, hopefully for good, without clearly having much long-term success.

One of the best strategies our inner skippers use to try to gain control of the vessel is to *solidify their position either by fear or hope, pain or pleasure, perceived social approval or perceived social rejection.* Each voice focuses on building an all-encompassing vision of existence and each voice does its best to run with it for the hopes of survival and permanence. These voices do run with it. They establish beliefs, axioms, frameworks and structures in an attempt to solidify a form of self illusion, which is, in essence, quite unstable and inevitably ends up appearing to be unsustainable sooner or later.

For example, in the mornings, we may be afraid of the future, uncertain of our past decisions, and maybe cautious of our feelings. By mid-day, we may be focused, efficient and getting our deadlines met. By the afternoon, we may be tired, wondering about the past, second-guessing our career path and by night, we may be empowered, fully confident, not taking negativity from anyone, centered and feeling in love with life. Also, these different conditions of self tend to repeat, sometimes in a consistent manner or sometimes in an inconsistent manner, depending on the internal landscape. Our midday skipper one day can grab the night shift another day and our morning skipper can be somewhat consistent for a while. Some aspects of certain skippers may be somewhat more consistent and be experienced in long-term cycles of maybe months, years or even decades.

Given this situation, it is only natural that at some point or another, many of us may wonder about this overall strange, contradictory, cyclical and at times profoundly confusing experience that we generally tend to take for granted. This is where we find again the consistent and natural by-product of Structural Interpretation: Suffering. In other words, *suffering is the effect of our several different inner voices trying to take control of our experience.* These voices interpret our situation from different angles, hoping to achieve an evidently unattainable unified experience. Unfortunately, this can result in losing all the energy invested in one particular interpretation of self only to have to endlessly start to build up, defend, maintain and sustain who we think we are, again and again, to inevitably see it shift again and again.

In the end, as counter-intuitive as this may sound, *there is no solid self in and of itself.* Therefore, there is no central I, there is no central me; there is no myself, rather, just a loosely arranged amalgamation of independent internal perceptions managing to appear to become a consistent and solid entity some of the time. In essence, *self, as we hope to experience it, is an innocent construction on our part.* This is the reason why I will use the term *self-illusion* rather than sense of self, me or I to express this experience of apparent internal grounding. In particular, I will not be referring to "sense of self" because it has a clear and appropriate meaning in other disciplines along with the term "self-esteem", often referring to the healthy and necessary developmental process in children and adolescents as they physically and emotionally adapt to their environment. These themes are clearly not in the scope of this book.

It is very important not to objectify or personify self-illusion in any way. *In essence, self-illusion is clearly not something or someone in particular.* This is actually the point of the illusion. Rather, self-illusion should be understood simply as a mirage, as a *perceptional illusion* in the same way we experience *optical illusions*. Therefore, as self-illusion resolves, we actually do not loose anything (because there was nothing there in the first place) while at the same time we become complete.

The extraordinary news is that our confusion and effort resolve when we finally experientially realize that if there is actually no central or unified self. Our tension and urgent search also then dissolves. Even more extraordinarily, we find that where there is no illusory self, there is no suffering, no stress, no loss, no dread and no fear. *Without an illusory self, there is only open, pristine and all-sustaining space.*

This is a state that allows for extraordinary flexibility, unattached joy, unconditional love, compassion and an all-encompassing experience of freedom and wellbeing that is beyond polarization, language, attachment and form. *The fact that there is no illusory central self opens the door to our ultimate emancipation and liberation from both al-*

ternating positions of the dualistic experience and opens the door to the ultimate adventure. It opens the door to a continuous experience of undivided presence that rests within itself and is sustained by itself, yet it is not separated from anything else.

2

Understanding

In all your promises,
there has never been such clarity.
In all your territories,
there has never been such space.
In all your labyrinths,
there has never been such light.

The three answers to the seven kingdoms
are found in the uninhabitable space,
in the cell that holds nothing,
on the grounds of non-conception,
in the absence of the opposites,
All clarity,
perfect.

The Language
Paradox

Language is as universal as human suffering (Hayes, 2005). It is everywhere. In our minds, in our breath, in our tongues, on our streets, in our books, in the moral codes we hold, in the letters of love and longing we write as well as in the countless expressions of joy, hope, agony and loss we experience as human beings. Language is in the exaltation of the sublime as well as in the cursing struggle of damnation. Interestingly enough, if we look at it closely, language and suffering go hand in hand. Wherever one is present, the other naturally follows. The reason for this complicity is that, in essence, *language is a highly limited tool when it comes to the expression, embodiment, communication, sustainment and comprehension of Being as a profound human experience. Therefore, whenever we use it for these purposes, it constantly falls short in achieving its goal.*

Language is an enormous accomplishment. Nevertheless, we do not have any other alternative for communication or a more sophisticated way to conceptually build the world we live in. Yet, we seem to consistently experience that language does not truly express what we are experiencing at deeper levels, and we notice how endlessly problematic this process is, given how often we get in trouble when using it. Adults as well as kindergarten children find themselves perplexed when addressed with the questions: Why did you say that? What do you mean by that? What are you trying to say? This is because all human beings, regardless of stature or education, seem to struggle to convey their experience of Being through language, given that *applying language to phenomena reflected in consciousness-as-mirror at a profound level actually diminishes our experience of Being.* In other words, language ends up being a mental abstraction of Being itself, and as such, it cannot contain Being in and of itself. It cannot sustain the existential demands that we tend to impose on it, thus generating a considerable inner void that in turn creates *a profound sense of separation.*

This is the case because language is based on a very simple dualistic principle of consistent categorization, oscillating between opposites, identifying existence and non-existence – a dualizing process that happens between being and nonbeing, as well as the subsequent categorizations of endless levels, shades, grades and differences between these two basic dual principles. Being can in no way be remotely encompassed in language and polarization; language is not a sustained or wholesome reflection of Being, even though we may appear to be convinced of this. Being could never, in its purity, vastness and complexity, be reliably embodied, communicated or expressed by language.

Language clearly has an unparalleled role when it comes to communication, knowledge, science, research, academia, exploration and relationships. It is also crucial when it comes to organization, safety and interaction or as a signaling point towards form and its endless expressions. Language becomes particularly handy when we need help, directions, sustainment or as a way out of a life threatening or a difficult situation. Language may also serve a purpose by addressing its own limitations and hence, pointing towards the door into Curflexion. As we will explore further we will see that this is the case in this book. Nevertheless, *the bottom line is that Being cannot be fully sustained in a naturally dualistic structure such as language and the subsequent polarization that comes with it.*

This in no way means that we should entirely give up on language, ditch it completely and run to a cave, even though it may very well be a preference for some who find the perils of language particularly unmanageable. What I believe to be of unsurpassable importance is to be *really clear of language's profound limitations* coupled with our consistent tendency to consider language as a reliable reflection or a vehicle of Being, in and of itself, demanding the impossible of it.

If we were to extend language to the realm of internal images, thoughts, or emotions, we would basically see that in most cases, this would include mostly our entire internal human experience at the level of self-illusion. If Being cannot be fully expressed through language and polarization, it also cannot be expressed through thoughts and emotions. *Thoughts, emotions, and language are the foundational building blocks of self-illusion as well as the building blocks of all possible forms of conceptualization, dualization, and, therefore, a clear source of instability and oppositional suffering.*

No wonder we seem confused, and no wonder we cannot seem to stop suffering. When it comes to the dimension of Being, it is as if a machine has been running a protocol that uses most of the machine's resources only for the purposes of sustaining the same protocol and is not producing anything outside of running the same protocol. In this case, the machine has no energy or capacity left for anything else, producing a constant and underlying struggle to solve or get out of a difficult situation by using the same tools in the same way that established and propelled the original condition in the first place, while strengthening and prolonging this situation consistently into the future.

By building up our internal universe with language, thoughts, emotions, and concepts, we are actually filling up the space of Being with enough clutter to lose sight of Being and convince ourselves that the clutter we see is *actually Being itself.* We are constantly attempting to build up solutions by using concepts and language with the intent to solve our inner entrapment, which we now know is constituted of concepts and language as well, perpetuating the original situation we are in, basically feeding debris into more debris and making it more difficult to get out.

As the primordial expression of who we are, Being lies consistently and reliably beyond the discourse, the noise, and the distraction within. From time to time, we sense Being as a profound intuition. Even when we experience the intuition of Being calling from within, when we look inside, we still tend to see the debris and end up interacting with the clutter, given that there is so much of it. We are not used to identifying the space that sustains everything behind the clutter, and we tend to take it for granted to the point that we cannot see it anymore.

Not really knowing where this profound call is coming from, we easily get distracted and start to innocently play around with mental forms. In this play, we may be hoping that through some particular arrangement of this clutter, some precise combination, some clear sequencing, some structuring, some form of opposition, some method, some fixing, some will, some form of accumulation, some level of dedication or intensity, or some secret or unique piece of clutter, we can embody the extraordinary radiance that exists only when we are *free of clutter.*

When we profoundly assimilate this paradox at a deep experiential level, and we let go of our constant internal expectations and demands for language and polarization to resolve our human condition or to eliminate our internal experience of suffering, *we naturally enter a dimen-*

sion of existence that is fully understanding, flexible, inclusive, compassionate, and entirely self-sustainable. We then naturally relax into an entirely welcoming disposition of our human experience: one where the immanent warmth and clarity of Being innately fills our entire perceptional space; one where our attention now inherently rests in the exquisite space of life that radiantly manifests precisely where we are.

The 2-for-1 Paradox

One of our most perplexing and unnoticed conditions as human beings is that without knowing it, every time we buy into a *positive* thought, emotion, or circumstance in order to counter a *negative* internal experience, we are actually also buying into its negative experience (Hayes, 2005) as well as into an unavoidable cyclical entrapment. It is important to note that we are actually buying into the negative experience at the exact same time and in the exact same moment we are originally buying into the positive, even if the actual effect comes later. *It is as if we paid in advance for both experiences while only wanting one of them.* I call this the 2-for-1 Paradox.

No wonder why the multiple self-help strategies and methodologies we may have attempted in the past most probably have consistently failed to produce the results we were expecting. The reason for this is that when we invest energy into a positive thought or experience with the intention to counter a negative thought or experience, we are inadvertently solidifying the future experience of a more intense negative thought or experience as well. As you think, support, and sustain a positive internal influence, you end up promoting, focusing on, defending from, and therefore, also solidifying the negative influence you are trying to move away from (Hayes, 2005). Even more, as you can imagine, *we are inadvertently solidifying a self-perpetuating cycle*, given that the moment we buy into the positive, we actually pay in advance for the negative as well. When we end up experiencing the negative, we will then buy into the positive again, and in doing so, we will be paying in advance for the negative one more time, and so on, and so forth.

In our internal world, thoughts and emotions have the endless spawning ability of mythical characters that have endless lives, but the caveat is that it is also one where their enemies enjoy the exact same perpetual life-spawning privileges. So, in an environment of endlessly spawning positive forces fighting against endlessly spawning negative forces, we would find ourselves in an endless battle of infinite spawning dual positions fighting for supremacy without knowing that this same fight actually feeds both sides and makes them equally stronger, even if at times, one side appears to be winning over the other.

Indeed, at times, it may appear that there is some stability of the light overcoming darkness, and we may very well think that we finally have arrived to wherever we think we should be able to find some kind of permanent happiness or stability. It does not matter how much we have attempted to solidify the positive and eradicate the negative; the negative will come back as part of this cycle, feeding an endless self-perpetuating spiral. *This is clearly an unwinnable situation.*

This cycle seems to be self-perpetuating and very difficult to stop, but it is also very difficult to notice as an issue mainly because we have been socialized to experience it as a natural part of life or even as life itself, yet, while at the same time, not being aware of the repetitive and paradoxical nature of its entrapment. *It is clear that seeking the negative in order to obtain the positive will also not work* because what we are buying into is not only the initial negative to obtain a final and stable positive, but we are actually buying into an *endlessly perpetuating cycle of dualities* that naturally produces tension and suffering.

The more we fight depression with positivity, the more depressed and lonely we end up feeling, and the cycle will continue. The more insistent we are on finding love, the more lonely and separated we will end up feeling, only to find love again, and then loneliness again. If we own a house, we are now immediately concerned with caring for it and maintaining it. If we have money, we are now invested in not losing it. If we own a car, we are now concerned with its longevity and reliability. Interestingly enough as well, no amount of ownership has ever produced the end of this dualistic conundrum. Everything we own, we can lose, and therefore, the pain of loss is always a by-product of ownership. Every time we agree to fidelity, we have to address and deal with the confusion, pain, and fear of infidelity; every time we address security issues, we have to deal with the fear of insecurity and exposure. So, no amount of rigid expectations will ever provide us with the safety, internal peace, and control we are expecting from originally establishing these expectations.

In this same way, righteousness constantly battles and feeds our own shame. The more righteous we feel, the less space we allow ourselves for learning, experimentation, and failure and the more judgmental we become of ourselves and others. Rigidity takes us away from peace, no matter how hard we try to eradicate chaos. The more we try to control or eradicate chaos, the more dualities of anxiety and shame we will experience. Generally speaking, we feel righteous when we are convinced we are doing the right thing. However, if we come to deeply know that what we stand for now may change tomorrow because there is no permanent, central self and that what we dread today, we may happily embrace tomorrow, we may want to choose to remain somewhat more flexible from the start.

Identifying and assigning value and counter value seem to be a deeply entrenched human endeavor that has produced consistently contradictory results and, at times, even random outcomes throughout history. We often forget that the expectations we currently take for granted and to be self-evident are only the consensual interpretation of the times. Fears and hopes for humanity are established as behavioral expectations through self-referenced processes that are laid on the dichotomy of a dualistic experiential approximation based on particular forms of language, thought, and emotion. These fears and hopes then get explicitly or implicitly established as expectations without any form of actual grounding in Being, given that Being does not discriminate anything by definition and, at the same time, sustains and welcomes everything.

When we establish an expectation, we assume that we have established the conditions that will allow us to follow the expectation without considering that *the expectation is actually summoning and strengthening its own counter expectation*. So, in essence, when we establish expectations, we are not really preventing something; *rather, we are promoting that exact same thing we are trying to prevent*, which promotes a self-sustaining dualistic cycle and further suffering without any foreseeable end.

In order to eliminate suffering, *we need to let go of the entire original two-way buy-in process by which we are constantly thrown into these cycles of opposites*. We need to find a way to remain de-dualized and neutrally independent of what is actually making us buy into one of the two opposites in this dualistic condition. We need to become the space that holds both positions rather than identifying with one particular position while rejecting or fighting the other one.

This does not mean we should become disengaged, non-responsive, depressed, passive-aggressive, inattentive, or emotionally detached. On the contrary, our current suffering condition calls for engagement, responsiveness, and aliveness, as we interact with what manifests every moment in a way that is free from want, rejection, and projection and is fully welcoming and non-discriminating —a way that is open, inclusive, and complete; a way where nothing is internally lacking; one where there is no waiting; and one where there is no separation or isolation.

As we profoundly integrate and assimilate the 2-for-1 Paradox, our impulse to fix or manipulate out internal suffering experience simply ceases. As this happens, *we gently and naturally move into a space of fully welcoming the experience we are being presented with, every second of every day,* without any need for this experience to be any different than it is. In this way, *our sense of separation dissolves* and our need for internal defense evaporates, resulting in a profound and immanent connection with Being-As-Is —a connection with the exquisite and radiant energy of life that supports us and that doesn't need anything else, at any time, to be complete.

The Nowhere to
Settle Paradox

As you may have clearly noticed by now, this is not a traditional dualistic approach to addressing confusion in our lives. In other words, I will not be offering you a recipe on how to finally fix and triumph over confusion, loss, and depression, replacing them by the things we cherish most such as hope, love, and pleasure. *There is no way to successfully address our human condition by fighting the endless battle of the opposites.* The practices I will share with you later on in this book have nothing to do with winning the ever-spawning internal war of opposites. These practices will be an invitation to move from the entrapment of self-illusion and its ongoing impossible hope for existence and permanence, into the fluid, ever-present, naturally compassionate, self-continuing, and self-sustaining embodiment of Being-As-Is.

Going back to the vessel analogy, the Nowhere to Settle Paradox presents the idea that further to somehow temporarily amassing control, our *skipper in turn* will now additionally need to face yet another insurmountable challenge. This challenge is, that after all the cajoling, strategizing, convincing, polarizing, identifying and solidifying needed in order to establish leadership over other competing voices, in the end, and after all that work, *our skipper in turn will not be able to find a solid, reliable, and consistent platform to reify and sustain its leadership.*

Indeed, self-illusion seems to be constantly seeking to internally settle in some form of safe and permanent definition or container of itself, somewhere where it can definitely say "I am this" or "I am that" or "My life is about this" or "I stand for that." It is seeking a place where it can consistently say me, my, I, or mine and comfortably rest there for good. Interestingly enough, at this point, it would be easy to see that this space is simply and surprisingly nonexistent.

There are all kinds of possible goals or potential settling platforms for self-illusion, with countless grades, shades and possibilities. By now, it would be easy to see that the traditional settling platforms for self-illusion, which we generally falsely perceive to be the safeguards of our internal experience, have two inherent fundamental flaws: abstraction and dualization. Every time self-illusion tries to define, solidify, or validate itself as a consistent entity, *it is attempting to settle somewhere solid enough to sus-*

tain itself. *When this happens, without knowing it, self-illusion will also be instantly buying into the eventual dissolution of that same experience.* As a matter of fact, given that there is no actual solid self, then in essence, there is no possible permanent platform for self as well.

We often think that our main problem resides in finding the ideal platform to settle in for good. Some of these platforms we are searching for may be ones such as finding our soul mate, getting the perfect job, finding a perfect partner, experiencing the ultimate solution of some kind, or achieving enlightenment or spiritual realization. There are also more rebellious illusory platforms that would seem to support nonconformist approaches. Anything that implies validation, reification, or solidification of self-illusion is, in itself, a settling platform regardless of the style, theme, or type of rendering it may have.

In truth, any dualistic position *will be impossible to achieve in a sustained and solid way.* Not because there is still something missing in the conceptualization, understanding, or construction of the internal settling spot, nor because it needs better foundations, nor because it lacks the ultimate secret ingredient, material, or treasure, not because we lack the confidence, self-assurance, or commitment we think we need, but because *there is no one to actually settle.* There is no central self. There is just a rambunctious group of skippers doing their best to get hold of our vessel's helm wheel without any possibility of success.

Even though finding the perfect and final platform to settle may have been an engraved goal since we were initially convinced that there was something wrong with us that needed fixing, be it whatever this platform may be for each one of us, *settling is simply impossible by definition because there is no central self.*

This doesn't mean that there is no point to existence and that life has no purpose; it only means that what we thought life was about might actually be an honest mistake given that it is simply impossible for self-illusion to settle anywhere. *Actually, this true inability to settle is our best proof that self-illusion is non-existent, empty, and without consistency or identity.* We simply cannot rest in any solid platform, and therefore, *we do not exist as we think we do.* Existence, as we know it through self-illusion, is something that needs to be *sustained, defended and maintained.* Being, on the other hand, simply exists and manifests *without our manipulation.*

When we profoundly assimilate and integrate the Nowhere to Settle Paradox, we let go of our constant struggle to define and solidify who we think we are. As we do this, *we are imbued with an exquisite experience of spaciousness and peace that is completely self-sustaining* and has nothing to do with our pre-conceived notions of these ideas. It is also fully independent of any external conditions and situations we may be presented with in our daily life. The spaciousness that emanates from this integration, interestingly enough, also provides us with an exquisite sense of grounding and complete trust in Being-As-Is that has no comparison to any possible experience at the level of self-illusion. As we allow ourselves to fully embody the infinite space of Being, through the profound understanding and embodiment of the Nowhere to Settle Paradox, our internal experience of suffering naturally resolves.

3

Deconstruction

The edifice of self-illusion
dissolves into all-sustaining space.

Through rubble, dust, and thundering roar, or
through the sweet melody of the enlightened flute,
we will come through the door of freedom!

Dancing around,
while completely contained
in open, endless space.

Dissolution

Behind our mental noise, it is very probable we all have the intuition that there is nowhere to internally settle, nowhere to take refuge and nowhere to solidify self-illusion. This is an intuition that whispers in our ear, sharing with us that it does not matter how hard we try, how thoroughly we endeavor to convince ourselves, or how much we invest, self-illusion cannot settle and comfortably rest anywhere. This may be the original cause of all the evidently pointless running around in which we humans engage. We seem to have conceptualized and internalized that death is inevitable and that in the meantime, there is nowhere to feel secure or complete. Somewhere deep inside, we all seem to know that there is nowhere to hide.

This intuition of non-self seems to demand an enormous amount of distraction in order to make our situation bearable given the apparent level of confusion and contradiction we sometimes inhabit. Addictive entertainment seems to be ubiquitous to dualistic human experience. Anything that would allow for us to become distracted from the intuition that there is actually nowhere to settle and no one to settle with has the potential to gain enormous momentum and commercial success.

Distraction is endemic to humans and has now been coated with a layer of lifestyle and enjoyment that has convinced many people that this is precisely what we are all about: that life is precisely about the many distractions, the quality of the distractions, the longevity of the distractions, the intensity of the distractions or the refinement of the distractions; apparently, the more distractions, the better.

The *Nowhere to Settle Paradox* intuition concerns self-illusion a great deal. *For self-illusion, the Nowhere to Settle Paradox actually implies simple unsustainability.* If we pair this perception with the eventual inevitable dissolution of the human body, we would just need a nice red ribbon to package and solidify our main source of fear in this world. Dualistic confusion also helps with the delivery of this nicely ribboned package by assuming that *if there is no place to internally settle, then this must mean that there is no place to live* and hence, that there is no point in living, giving way to nihilism and pessimism - nothing could be further from the truth.

Dissolution of self-illusion has been a long-used analogy throughout history when it comes to finding out who we truly are. In many traditions, it is not until we let go of who we believe we are completely and utterly that we can find who or what we truly are. Losing everything before regaining clarity and insight of our true nature or Being is indeed a constant theme in the history of human-kind, one that is used to illustrate this point in particular.

It is important to note that the Language Paradox, the 2-for-1 Paradox, as well as the Nowhere to Settle Paradox are actually doors into resolving the illusion of self (i.e., the process that will allow for the cessation of suffering as well as the entrance into the ever-present space of Being). Who hurts if there is no one to hurt? Who dies if there is no one to die? Who suffers if there is no one to suffer? Who loses if there is no one to lose?

If we know that (a) every time we polarize something, we are limiting our expression of Being; or if we know that (b) every time we buy into something, we are being tricked into buying its cyclical opposite; or if we know that (c) no matter how hard we try, we will not be able to internally settle anywhere, because there is actually no one who needs settling, we may naturally want to abstain from this madness.

For example, if we know that every time we attempt to solidify self-illusion in some form of permanent refuge, it will result in a crash-landing, we may prefer to stay up in the air, we may prefer to stay in the space of all freedom and possibilities rather than in concrete confusion. *No polarization, no buying into and no solidification are the quintessential doors to Curflexion.* This means that with those three essential pitfalls out of the way, we may finally experience the openness, vastness, compassion and inclusiveness of Being fully as we let go of the traditional suffering of opposition and instability that seems to constantly get in the way.

Depression

It is quite common for individuals to go through mild or severe cases of existential confusion as a result of dealing with life issues that can easily lead to several forms of depression (Burton, 2010). In my experience, *some forms of depression derive from a profound experience of internal resistance, a form of resentful indignation or a deep existential complaint about the instability and unreliability of self-illusion.*

Some of these cases may come as a result of our constant unsuccessful attempts to reduce Being to language, dualization or solidification. When we seem to not get what we want (essentially the solidification and safety of self-illusion) at a very profound level, we sometimes tend to experience a deep sense of defeat, fear, loss or threat. This situation often produces a sense of dread through the perceived potential risk of dissolution of self-illusion. Of course, I am not referring to all cases of depression. Many cases may be clearly beyond the scope of this book. As stated in the introduction of this book, individuals should seek appropriately qualified, licensed and professional support to address their particular needs.

Fortunately, depression holds enormous transformational potential (Burton, 2010). In some cases, it actually holds the potential to allow Curflexion to manifest within. In an individual's life experience, depression may be a sign of the emergence or ripening of the understanding of one, two, or three (or a combination) of the paradoxes (the Language Paradox, the 2 for 1 Paradox and the Nowhere to Settle paradox). Depression can be the dawning of the existential realization that we will never be able to attain solid grounding for self-illusion and this realization can present itself in a myriad of different forms or scenarios for different people. This realization can be difficult to process in some cases, particularly for individuals who do not have the experience or guidance to transform these forms of depression into a liberating experience.

When we arrive to the profound realization that there is no possible negotiation, no silver bullet, no soul mate, no perfect arrangement and no law that can ever make our unrealistic hopes, needs and wants of self-illusion a reality in the way that we desire, yes we may indeed become depressed: sometimes mildly, sometimes severely.

Self-illusion feeds from the same energy of separation, confusion, anticipation, elation, hope, expectation and projection that we produce when we polarize, differentiate, label, pursue better for worse and affirm that we are something or other. When we realize the illusory nature of this proposition and the edifice of self begins to soften, we may certainly experience confusion at times, especially when we lose sight of Being.

In these cases, self-illusion can be quite persuasive. Hence, it does what it can to convince us not to pursue the road towards cessation and liberation. Self-illusion will attempt to do this through worry, stress or fear. Even when this is the case, it is important to remind ourselves that these experiences are also only illusory platforms that we will be presented with in order to solidify an unreal perception of solid existence. *It is very important to remember that these experiences are exactly as nonexistent as self-illusion, given that they are actually produced by self-illusion in order to solidify its own illusory self-existence.*

The profound realization that our experience of a central self is an illusion is the door to our final destination and our final liberation from confusion. So, the fact that our internal world may be softening or dissolving on its own through some form of depression may be an extraordinary opportunity to experience Curflexion. In doing so we are presented with the opportunity to move forward and learn how to live in a space without polarization, without seeking to solidify the impossible.

At the same time, depression is definitely not a necessary prerequisite towards embodying ultimate freedom. For some individuals, the experience of Curflexion can manifest after a soft and gentle road as their illusory self gently resolves. In these cases, the individuals will unthread slowly and consistently, allowing space, understanding, and compassion to flow freely around them. It is important not to assume that there is a right way and a wrong way to allow for the unraveling of Curflexion to manifest in our lives. For these individuals, Curflexion may unravel as the tender tune of a flute on a fresh, sunny afternoon, while sipping lemongrass tea with honey. For others, Curflexion may unravel as the unexpected dissolution of everything they imagine to be real. There is no correct way to proceed, there is no standard experience and there is no particularly prescribed path or sequence. Each of us has our own path.

Death

As noted before, self-illusion strives to solidify its existence through conceptualization, polarization, separation and rationalization; through defending the perception of dualization and through reifying the idea of who we think we are. Self-illusion seems to build castles in the sky out of thin air with imagined pins, needles and string that are also made up of thin air – all this in order to validate its own existence. *The idea of the dissolution of something that cannot be dissolved because it does not actually exist, drives most of what we do* in the form of direction, anxiety, drive, stress and even subtle tension, sometimes presenting us with the gift of our own great existential complaint or depression, which brings with it the great potential to access Curflexion.

We may want to ask: What about the actual dissolution of our human form? What about the death of our body? Well, a good initial approximation to address this question could be asking ourselves, *"What would death and dying be if there was nothing to hold onto in the first place?"* If there is no one in here, then who dies? Understanding this phenomenon at a deep experiential level allows for a profound and lasting experience of liberation, peace and completeness that is incomparable to any dualistic experience of peace.

Physical death is as common to existence as is birth, suffering and language. Death is all around us all the time and the thought of death is a continual visitor in our internal world. It may be our death or other people's death, but it is certain that death is truly alive in us. It is really interesting to explore why we are so averse to death given that it is so common. We are not averse to breathing or eating or walking; but we do have issues with death.

If we understood death to be some kind of pain-inflicting experience, we would certainly try to avoid it. Even if this were the case, there would not be many alternatives to its inevitability. Pain is not a deterrent of experience. If it were, the human race would have disappeared long ago through the anticipation of childbirth. Human beings endure physical or psychological pain in very efficient ways. So if pain is not our concern when it comes to death, what is? Why are we so afraid to die? Why do we seem to dread it so much? Anticipate it so much? Reject it so much? The answer is simple. *Death seems to be such a problem to us particularly because it means the dissolution of self-illusion.*

Our illusory self literally battles its own self-interpretation of non-existence. That is mainly what it appears to do all the time that it is on duty, which is most of the time, with the exception of our experience of sleep without dreams. It battles non-existence at all levels and all times, while it is running its own show precisely because it does not exist in its own right. Because of this, it needs to consistently build itself up in order to attempt to manifest. For that to happen, it also needs to invest copious amounts of energy, effort and stress into its validation and relevance in order to convince, peddle and cajole for its own existence. If self-illusion existed in its own right and carried true existential weight, there would be no need to spend energy trying to justify, validate, support and nurture its own existence.

True existence rests in a form that is beyond doubt because of its own weight and evidence. There is no need to justify, argue, defend or validate anything that exists in order for it to exist. It either does or it does not. True existence is silent. True existence is complete. True existence is atemporal. True existence never dies, even if its manifestation disappears. It never dies because even when it is no more, there is still no lack, still no fault, still no sense of being incomplete and still no expression of inadequacy.

True existence is the most humble of manifestations, yet it will not cater to or validate the dreams of others. True existence cannot be argued with because there is no doubt within true existence. When engaged, true existence will reply with a kind and silent metaphorical smile or a flexible, inclusive, open, honest and engaged process of exploration into the nature of its stability and reliability.

Death is again, in the end, an abstraction of mind fuelled by thought, language and emotion. It is the most powerful trick available to self-illusion in order for it to be able to constitute, validate and sustain itself as apparently real and worthwhile. *Therefore, self-illusion invests considerable energy into the illusory idea of death in order to validate its own illusory idea of existence.*

True existence does not need death to justify itself. Being needs no justification, no defense, no exaltation and no strategy. Completeness has no opposite and endless space has no limit. Death, as we know it, does not exist because there is no self that actually dies or in other words, the self that apparently dies is not Being itself, but an illusory construction in our mind that consumes most of our energy in order to sustain and validate itself.

One of the main strategies self-illusion uses to validate itself is to summon the fear of the opposite, in this case, the opposite to its own illusory existence, which is illusory non-existence or, in other words, death as we know it. In perceiving this, we deeply understand that existence requires no validation and no projection, no hope and no expectation. In this case, death is simply unnecessary, becoming an absolute non-issue. When physical death arrives in the realm of Being, it simply arrives as Being itself: full, complete and without a need for anything else. No need for life, no need for action, no need for want and no need for hope. In which case, death is perfectly sustained and perfectly contained. Therefore *it does not need life to be complete.*

Death is only sustainable as an issue in the space of dualistic experience and an absolute non-issue when it comes to the space of Curflexion. In the endless space of Curflexion, death is nothing more than a legend propagated and propelled by self-illusion hoping to use it as a leverage for solidifying itself. When we are able to see the apparition for what it is, the construct dissolves and we arrive home for good.

Free Will

Free will seems to be an illusion in the same way self seems to be an illusion. In other words, we are not free in the way we generally believe ourselves to be (Harris, 2012). Questioning the existence of free will may generate the same pause as pondering the non-existence of self. When it comes to our social consensual understanding, the majority of us discard anything that may suggest lack of freedom hence, tampering with self-illusion. Our illusory self seems to need to feel free in order to convince itself that it can actually settle somewhere and sustain itself in some form or another. Interestingly enough, this may indeed be one of the most intriguing misconceptions of the human condition.

Self-illusion needs the notion of free will as much as it needs the notion of death to validate its own illusion of existence. It is important to clarify that *freedom can definitely be embodied in the vast space of Being,* nevertheless, in this space, freedom looks, feels, tastes and is experienced in a completely different way than what we experience freedom as at the level of self-illusion. The freedom that comes from Curflexion is the kind of freedom that comes from allowing Being, rather than opposing what we believe is negative with the forces we believe to be positive.

Self-illusion can add all kinds of apparently unfortunate labels to any notion of absence of free will, but it is especially important to remember that all of these labels are dualistic concepts that manifest when self-illusion settles on the concept or platform of *lack of free will*. Freedom, beyond the interpretation of self-illusion, should be understood more as an *allowing of existence at every moment*, rather than as a limitation. It can be understood as one of *endless possibilities*, rather than the seeking of a particular, desired outcome. Freedom should be understood as an experience of *spaciousness* and *flexibility* rather than one of strategy and manipulation.

If it is true that we do not employ free will at the dualistic level of self-illusion, then who actually runs the show? Well, let us explore this question. How much control do you have over the fact that you were born? Or over when and where you were born? How much control do you have over your gender? Over your height? Over the colour of your eyes or skin? Over the fact that some beings, walk, others fly and still others crawl? None. None whatsoever. All these foundational conditions of our existence are predetermined and at the same time, these are the preconditions of further conditions, which are also the preconditions of our current state, all the way to the thought that appeared in your mind right now. Even our entrenched belief in the illusion of free will is the result of an endless line of conceptual assumptions that work to sustain self-illusion rather than Being-As-Is. What appears to be the proof supporting free will is only an effect of an endless series of causes that actually leave little room for freedom. *Free will at the level of self-illusion is but a mirage that serves self-illusion to openly engage in its endless illusory pursuit of solidification and validation.*

You may ask who is then deciding to read these words? Who decided to write this book? Who is pondering these ideas and experiencing these internal forms? As we have seen before, sense-making is a self-sustaining construct that appears to have solid existence, but it is composed of a combination of loosely arranged voices that do their best to appear as one solid entity, a process that becomes a self-perpetuating cycle of giving and taking away meaning, understanding and confusion.

If you take the time to notice what is actually happening while you read this book, you will notice that as I write, I am simply inviting you to move from the realm of form into the realm of infinite space. This is what is happening, section after section. The result of this is that you either do it or you do not do it. When you actually do it as opposed to when you do not is predetermined by the same endless line of causes and preconditions that made you pick up this book. These same causes and preconditions are now allowing you to read up to this page and now this particular word, and this one, and now this one. All other apparent meaning, or strategy, or movement or expectation is simply perceptional and non-substantial: in other words, illusory. There is absolutely no way you could have not read this sentence after you have actually read it, and so it is with all that manifests in our lives.

We simply cannot entirely control what we experience in the present moment and we also could not have changed what has already happened in the past (Harris, 2012). We only seem to be able to either resist what is happening, or to allow and welcome that same thing that is happening. Absolutely everything that is not readily available in the present moment is, by definition, unachievable in the present moment; therefore, attempting to fix Being-As-Is through polarization, becomes a complete waste of time and energy. *Freedom at the level of Being manifests as we understand the fact that we are not as free as we generally think we are and so we let go of the tremendous effort and energy we invest in upholding the fantasy that we are free at the level of self-illusion.*

In our daily lives, it is clear that sometimes the expectations of self-illusion may match reality without any effort. Interestingly enough, in these cases, we tend to believe that we actually decided the outcomes as a product of our own effort, intelligence and of course, free will. Unfortunately, we generally experience this as a success only because we believe in the illusion that we produced the result ourselves, rather than the result was produced regardless of the play of our own self-illusion, then *internally assimilated as something wanted rather than something not wanted*. So what is actually happening is that Being is following its clear, fully-sustained path, while we play the game not only of having wanted what ended up happening, but also having produced what we think we wanted as a result of our efforts and through the power of our will.

Our limited experience of free will at the level of self-illusion does not mean that we are living some form of predetermined enslavement or that we need to submit blindly to someone or something else. *Decision-making can always manifest from the space of Being-As-Is as allowing, rather than decision-making from self-illusion through resistance, defense, or strategy.* When we say no from Being-As-Is, there is no doubt, there is no strategy and there is no defense; there is no search for polarized gain, or oppositional betterment, or hope. It may appear difficult to identify the difference between these two experiences at first and of course, when we have limited experience with Curflexion, it may certainly seem confusing. A simple, practical approximation may be to start allowing for some time before reacting to situations.

In order to allow for a yes or no to manifest from the space of Being-As-Is, as opposed to from the space of self-illusion, we need to allow for the oppositional and reactionary response to pass and then move deeply into our body in search for the foundational energy that requires no validation or justification, the energy that needs no construction, no strategy, no manipulation, no defense and al-low for it to be as is. *If a no, a yes, or a maybe or something else comes, it will come from this same space of grounding, compassion and clarity.* Silence may also come as a result of this exploration; a simple smile may also manifest, a ges-ture, a glance, a sigh, or a profound explanation. If this en-ergy comes from Being-As-Is, then even if it could be in-terpreted by an outside observer as the manifestation of de-fense or want, it will come with the inner grounding that wants nothing and refuses nothing. When we say no from self-illusion, it is easy to notice that we are defending some kind of settling platform in that specific moment, that we are defending some form of polarization and we know this because we are outside of the space of *triparadoxial under-standing* (the conjoined understanding of the Language Paradox, the 2-for-1 Paradox, and the Nowhere to Settle Paradox).

As stated before, ultimate freedom looks, feels and is experienced in a profoundly different way than what we experience as free will at the level of self-illusion. At the level of self-illusion, the illusion of freedom is experienced as an oppositional endeavor attempting to manipulate con-structs that are a result of other continual constructs and strategies that actually leave little room for freedom. The freedom we experience in Curflexion is a freedom that has absolutely nothing to do with our dualized circumstances; it is a freedom we experience regardless of our daily situa-tions. It is a profound experience of being grounded and in peace. It is a freedom that is not dependent on any previous cause or any previous condition or situation. It is wholly immanent, substantially uncaused and completely non-discriminatory.

Relationships

Socialization has always been considered a healthy component of human interaction. Agreed. It is said that through socialization, we support each other and validate who we are; we offer our gifts to others and allow for others to offer their gifts to us. We enrich our lives with other experiences and learn about other possibilities. Of course, all this is indeed wonderful, but what about the side of socialization that limits our understanding of the world, promotes rigidity and solidifies self-illusion through the need for validation and recognition, often generating shame and guilt as an effect of noncompliance? What about the side of socialization that promotes unhealthy relationships, fear of rejection, and compliance through manipulation?

How much of our socialization experience promotes, expects and validates polarization and solidification? How much do we overuse language in social circumstances? How hard do we work to settle self-illusion by using the validation and approval of others? Yes, we do these things and we do them often, opening up another important area of confusion and suffering.

This condition does not mean that we would need to run away from everyone and hide somewhere where we cannot be reached or where we cannot be exposed to all these solidifying agents. However, it does mean that in order to address suffering and its complications in this life, we need to address and explore socialization and relationships through the deep experiential understanding of the three paradoxes. As we do this, all kinds of possible realizations, clarifications or insights may manifest freely, naturally and harmoniously for us.

It is important to clarify that all defense, support or allegiance for or against socialization will not produce any expected lasting positive results. Our attempts to fix socialization will only further its grip and intensity, as well as our attempts to promote socialization as the culmination of human existence. This approach will only bring rigidity and inflexibility to our lives.

If it is not a matter of running from social life and it is not a matter of fighting against or fixing social life, then what do we do to address the suffering and confusion brought by socialization through the overuse of language, dualism and solidification? For starters, the answer is to *remain exactly where we are* and allow for the understanding of the three paradoxes to unfold. As this happens, any action that needs to be taken will become naturally evident and will manifest with clarity, love and understanding, devoid of any form of suffering or tension - as the action will actually be coming from a space of grounding in Being.

Socialization also includes one of the most challenging and rewarding dimensions of our human condition. This would be our close personal relationships: partners, children, parents, or siblings. This dimension of socialization is especially complex given we carry enormous expectations from this group of individuals as well as they from us. We appear to be convinced that these individuals should behave in specific ways that adhere to our particular values and expectations. In this way, we believe, that they show their consideration towards and care for us. It is easy to see that as we believe this of them, they also believe this of us.

We believe that relationships and their different expressions should be established and sustained under certain clear and consistent conditions: for example, that trust should be supported by certain clear guarantees or that fidelity should be seen and maintained in very particular ways or that love should always be expressed only in certain forms. As we all know, sooner or later, our expectations tend to not be fully supported by others in a consistent and reliable way, generating disillusionment and often heartache.

We generally place an enormous weight in our close personal relationships to build, sustain, and solidify self-illusion. Not only that, we also task our personal relationships with the seemingly impossible mandate *to give us the gift of a dense existence as a sign of their love or commitment to the relationship.* This as we now know is genuinely impossible.

We seem to choose to be a part of someone else's life or not to be a part of someone else's life based mainly on whether we feel they have the potential to support or not to support our self-illusion and whether we are willing and able to support their self-illusion in return. This is generally how we interpret *relationship love* at a very basic and primordial level. We *fall in love* because we believe we have found someone who sees us for who we *actually are*, what we *truly believe in* and so we feel seen, we feel valued and we feel complete through their eyes; yet most importantly, we feel we exist and at the same time, we are willing to validate their self-illusion in return for them validating ours.

We agree to validate another individual's self-illusion as long as the validation and the support for the affirmation of our own illusory existence is mutually sustained and enabled. We are asking that person to give us *substance* through their own eyes as well as consistent existence through their discourse, their thoughts and their emotions, hoping for a reliable and solid form of existence through their experience of ourselves. The reality is that, in some cases, if this mutually sustaining aspect of the relationship does not last, generally *the relationship does not last either.*

At the level of the *other*, we are always unsure if what we are going to do or say will actually build or, on the other hand, diminish our partner's illusory self, consistently creating uncertainty for both individuals in the relationship. Also, every illusory self somehow believes that whatever they need in order to be supported and validated should tend to be as plain and clear to others as is it to the original illusory self. In other words, other people should know what works or does not work for the illusory self in need of validation and justification. As we know from actual experience, this is substantially far from the truth.

Understanding that we are *all* exposed to the *same* illusion of trying to build and maintain self-illusion is one of the most important opportunities we may have to address our most difficult relationship issues. This is absolutely not to justify or validate any condition of abuse or aggression in relationships nor any doormat situation or form of repression. We simply hope to understand that everyone who sustains an illusionary self will be naturally immersed in a delusory interpretation of reality. In this case, the tendency will be to constantly attempt to settle and solidify who they think they are, who they think we are or we should be, in ways that may be intentionally or unintentionally harmful to others or ourselves.

It is important to realize that when it comes to relationships, there is no need to artificially act on anything coming from the discursive or conceptualized level of self-illusion. If we allow for triparadoxia to truly live within our hearts, all that ever needs to change will change naturally, gently, compassionately, without drama (at least without drama on your side) and with the full understanding that is sustained by the deep acknowledgement of Being. In this way, relationships become genuine, grounded, honest and valued for what they truly are, rather than for what they falsely construct, embellish, sustain, or condemn. If we need to modify our life's arrangements, we will modify our life's arrangements by giving ourselves entirely to Being not a second before or after than when we actually do. In this case, all expectation, projection, anticipation or manipulation are absolutely unnecessary and are sources of much suffering.

If we engage our close personal relationships while understanding that we tend to be overly reliant on language and polarization, we can then allow for silence and space to play more vital roles; if on the other hand, we engage our close personal relationships knowing that trying to fix them or trying to fix ourselves will only result in the perpetuation of a cycle of positive and negative attributes that will plunge us into further confusion, this realization can result in true genuine respect for who we are, who they are and what we all bring to this world without losing our precious time in trying to change the unchangeable. Also, if we let go of the tendency to solidify self-illusion or solidify self-illusion in others (which we especially do in a relationship if it helps solidify our own) and counter-intuitively try to remain open and flexible to our own experiences and the experiences of others, we may come to enjoy the ride with genuine appreciation, surprise and delight for whatever happens each and every day of our lives.

Supportive family environments are a great idea, but in reality, they do not manifest all the time. Divorce or separation may be considered generally to be unfortunate and unwelcome, yet considering that divorce accounts for approximately half of the statistics in partnerships, the negative idea we may have of the reasons for divorce has not stopped these from happening consistently throughout the history of relationships. Not only that, but we also seem to fail to notice separation and divorce as an extraordinary blessing in countless cases where this condition is allowed to positively flourish and sustain the space that is needed for Being to shine through in that particular situation.

We also fail to see that in the case of many relationships, couples or marriages, sometimes these arrangements naturally and gently *complete* themselves radiantly (notice, I did not use words such as end, finish, dissolve, terminate, etc.). These relationships simply and kindly do not manifest any longer. In this case, divorce or separation would be equivalent to the ending of a beautiful day, where there is no regret, no longing, no quarrel, no demand, no anger, no disillusionment, no disappointment and no contention. Just a full, profound and genuine appreciation for the myriad colors on the horizon at that time as well as the light of every second lived throughout that day. Relationships complete, marriages complete, paternity and maternity complete, mentorships complete, jobs complete, while also at the same time, love completes, understanding completes, grounding completes and adventure completes.

It is genuinely true that relationships and socialization do not need to change in disarray, anger, violence or confusion; they just simply do because our options seem to be deeply limited. We seem to be immersed in a world of judging opposites, in which if something is not good, then it must necessarily be bad; or if something is not moving up, then it must necessarily mean it is stuck or it is moving down; or if something is not giving me what I want, that must mean it is then taking it away from me. In this case, we fail to see the countless possibilities that remain between the two extremes of either being miserable with someone or being miserable apart. The combinations and possibilities are endless; they just require an open mind, a de-polarized mind, a mind that can remain open past the immediate dualistic impulses presented by self-illusion.

Different family arrangements, accommodations, responsibilities, roles, and so on are not readily available in our menu of options, given our tendency to dualize relationships and acquiesce to the standard social narrative. In all honesty, we have not sufficiently explored our alternatives and the countless ways and possibilities we have as human beings to express love, companionship, care, understanding, support, compassion and work together with the common goal to survive.

The focus to address relationship issues would then be not on change, transformation, indignation, resolution, action or retribution, but rather the focus would be on *understanding, allowing, acknowledging, letting go and grounding ourselves in the full experience of non-discursive Being* through the deep experiential understanding of triparadoxia. From there, we can again allow and support what gently and naturally needs to happen for Being to manifest in full participation of life, compassion, understanding and effortless sustainment.

Purpose

We seem to be searching for some form of ultimate inner discovery. We seem to be trying to find our passion and our clear direction in life. We are searching for the primordial reason to be alive, for our purpose in life. We may believe our true passion is not clear or if it is, then that it may be compromised by social norms, by relationships, commitments, work, responsibilities and all sorts of other life situations. Alternatively, we may be afraid of the implications of following our passion, be it because of the changes that it may imply, the commitment it entails or the breaking of previous commitments that may no longer be relevant, applicable or viable for us. *The essence of this problem for the majority of us is that regardless of how hard we try, we cannot seem to find our ultimate passion and direction in life.*

It is easy to see many individuals, who apparently seem to have found their passion in life, to be constantly plagued by doubt, anxiety and insecurity. In reality, in the majority of cases, it seems that after having searched incessantly and consistently for this ultimate purpose, we seem to come out somewhat empty handed. We may think we see it clearly at times, believe we have found it and made every possible effort to sustain it; nevertheless, after changing our course in life towards that particular direction, which we clearly and vehemently identified as our passion in life, we often find that later on we either doubt or even regret the decision we have taken. We may come to believe that the path taken was a mistake or that something happened that has further changed our purpose or passion in life. We can also come to believe that our purpose in life is indeed extraordinary, but that it could be just a bit better.

Why does it seem that our purpose in life is so difficult to embody? And when we have got it, why does it change? Why do we lose our direction and passion? Why do we end up in doubt of something that was so clear at a particular time? Well, *because there is no central and consistent inner experience of self.* As we have seen before, there is just an endless competition of internal voices trying to make the best argument possible and pretending to manifest a unifying and consistent experience we call self.

The center of who we are ("me" or "my passion" or "my thing" or "what I do") is actually substantially nonexistent. If it does appears to exist, it seems to certainly not be permanent and therefore, it is unreliable. If there is no unifying experience and hence no central self, then there is no such thing as a central or unified passion or purpose in life as we think we know it or as we expect it to be. *What we may actually be looking for when we are seeking to discover our passion or purpose in life is a final resting and solidifying platform for self-illusion.* Because we are actually profoundly empty of a unified self, then we are only swayed by different voices at different times and in different circumstances, even if a single voice or group of voices takes the helm for a long time. This is why we generally end up looking for something we do not have and even if we seem to achieve it, we would then tend to seek for something else.

This does not mean, again, that we should then turn off the distraction hub and discard life, but it would certainly be a suggestion to just turn off the distraction hub and then remain fully alive and open and see what happens beyond the resolving fantasy of self-illusion.

If a central self does not actually exist and if identifying our purpose or passion in life is precisely another way of trying to settle self-illusion in an illusory platform that will, of course, result in a crash landing, let us ask ourselves, "What would our life look like without trying to find our purpose or a passion in life?" If we allow ourselves to experience life without a particular passion or purpose, we may be deeply surprised by the fact that when we are not searching for a fantasy in the future or trying to fix our present confusion or past mistakes, *we end up finding all we need right in front of us* in the all-allowing space of Being. *This is where the magic actually happens.*

Living without a passion or purpose at the level of self-illusion allows us the opportunity to actually open up and *experience whatever manifests as perfect in every second of every day.* In this case, there is no lack, allowing for non-discrimination of our daily experience and for the full welcoming of whatever we encounter in the endless space of Being-As-Is. As we do this, we will be surprised to see that without trying, or fixing or attempting to manipulate our experience, but rather by allowing and surrendering to the ever-present, all-encompassing and sustaining force that fuels everything, our search for purpose and passion in life is replaced by an all-sustaining, all-welcoming, all-present profound realization of Being that makes our regular notions of passion and purpose in life pale in comparison.

4

Being

The castle is entirely new.
No trace of lines or corners.
Not a shut door in sight.

In all its magnificence,
there has never been such triumph!

It manifests freely when nothing can sustain it.
No grounding, no pillars, no foundation.
No history, no wars, no lovers!

In one single instant,
I find myself as no-self!
Perfect spontaneity.
In the grace of endless space.

I am free!

Oneness

The force that sustains everything is indivisible. The cycle of what we call life and death is indivisible. The dualities we refer to as day and night, high and low, near and far or happy and sad are actually indivisible regardless of the polarizations we have artificially learned, amassed, and produced since we began to attempt to conceptualize Being. Without a polarizing labeling system, without chasing positive and hence attracting negative and without settling options for self-illusion, we find that everything that manifests in Being does not actually exist as a duality. It necessarily cannot be catalogued in polarizing categories and can only exist in the endless, all-welcoming space where it manifests.

It is fairly clear that what is not supposed to happen does not happen in this world and what is supposed to happen, happens regardless of our projection of adequacy or inadequacy. Humans lead complicated lives, generally immersed in a constant perceptual struggle that causes confusion, harm and suffering; and that is quite difficult to solve. Relationships tend to be problematic, regardless of our willingness for harmony and the many social and economic advantages this harmony could bring.

Life is what it is, every second, non-negotiable, even if we think it is and the fact that we think it is negotiable in that moment is also non-negotiable as well. So, if we do not dualize or polarize reality, we are then left with the vast totality of whatever happens as one complete, indivisible and therefore, necessary manifestation only because of the fact that it actually exists. We can then say that *all experience is Being* because of the simple fact that it manifests as is and because it is allowed or supported by the living force behind all manifestation.

Absolutely everything that happens, every single word, every single breath, every single action, every single thought, every single emotion, every single form is essentially and fundamentally Being itself, regardless of our story or interpretation of it. Surrendering to the manifestation of life, as is, all of it, with its energy, with every single aspect of it, without settling self-illusion in a false platform, without seeking one kind of experience and pushing away other kinds of experience, without categorizing, allows for full and unabridged completeness. *This is how we know that everything that manifests is part of Being and therefore, everything that does not exist is inconsequential or irrelevant because of the simple fact that it doesn't exist.*

Now that we have clarified this false dichotomy, we can see that non-duality is the true nature of our existence and that differentiation and dualization are simple imagined constructs of our conditioned experience and a result of our own misunderstood entanglement with suffering. Dualism appears to be a logical approximation to address human suffering. It appears to be clearly logical because in our everyday lives, things do work that way and the result is that we can get results from using an opposing approach to our physical external problems. As shared previously, when it comes to our internal experience, the fact remains that after thousands of years of attempting to succeed through the use of oppositional approaches to internal events, we are no closer to eliminating our inner confusion and what seems to be a constant experience of suffering.

When we are presented with the profound experiential understanding of triparadoxia and we realize the neutrality or absence of polarized existence within our internal experience, we acknowledge the unity and the lack of separation that allows for a complete experience of Being-As-Is and hence, for the understanding that everything manifests because of the simple fact that it exists, in which case, duality dissolves of its own accord. Consequently, if there is no sustainment for self-illusion, then necessarily, there is also no differentiation. No differentiation implies no separation, no dualization, no settling and no confusion.

This expression of the undivided reality that we live in is always complete. It is complete every second of every day. It lacks nothing, it hopes for nothing, it dreads nothing and at the same time it allows for the complete manifestation of the exquisite force that sustains everything. It is all radiant and all welcoming. It presents no separation and it manifests in full harmony with our deepest experience of Being. It is indivisible, borderless and without opposites. It is One.

Accountability

An obvious question to address is around the issue of accountability, retribution, liability and responsibility. If Being allows and equally supports everything that manifests to exist and all duality dissolves of its own accord and given that no differentiation is actually self-sustainable, then what are we left with? Given the illusory nature of our self, can we then justify not taking any responsibility? Is this the end of order and a form of validation to harm others? Is this a justification to break the rules? Are we then doomed to chaos? *Definitely not.*

Curflexion is not a justification for irresponsibility or chaos; it is not a justification to let our constructions and projections live out freely. Curflexion is not allowing or fuelling want without restraint or without consideration for others. The non-dual nature of Being is certainly not a justification for crime, violence, abuse, genocide or torture.

Curflexion allows for the natural experience of Being to entirely resolve our sense of lack, separation and incompleteness, and therefore, we naturally wish and seek no harm to others. When we know we are complete, we then see there is no need to covet anything. We do not get in the way of others, we do not harm others and we do not interfere with their rights and property. On the contrary, as the understanding of triparadoxia manifests internally, we naturally let go and acknowledge that no solid internal posture can be sustained and because of this, we are unable to harm others in the process.

Harming others and ourselves actually comes from a lack of profound experiential understanding of triparadoxia. All intent to harm is an attempt to settle self-illusion in some form of conceptual solid grounding. All intent to harm comes from self-illusion hoping to achieve something. All intent to harm is a form of validation of self-illusion and therefore a form of false refuge. All harm comes from polarization and dualization. All harm comes from seeking something and rejecting its opposite. Triparadoxia and Curflexion imply a natural, profound and compassionate absence of harm through the deep experiential understanding of our reality.

If there is no one within, then there is absolutely no reason to harm anyone and no reason to covet anyone else's property because there is nothing to achieve given that there is no one to actually achieve anything. There is no gain through asserting self-illusion. When we know that self-illusion is nonexistent, we know that if we pay for or buy into what we think we want, we also pay in advance for what we think we do not want at the same time. Once we know that self-illusion has no safe space in which to hide and permanently solidify its experience of existence, then there is absolutely no motive, intent, desire or force to either break any rule, damage any property or harm anyone.

Believing that because there is no central self we are free to cause harm or that if there is no central self then we would not have to take responsibility for our actions is a disguised and misguided attempt on the part of self-illusion coming in through the back door to solidify and validate itself. If we were to buy into this argument, the part we would be missing is that 'being free to cause harm', or 'not having to take responsibility', are, in themselves, *assertions of self-illusion* and therefore self-illusion would actually be trying to use the abstract concept of its non existence to justify and validate its delusory existence, opening the door, once more, to yet another cycle of confusion and suffering.

In this particular case, first, we would be using language and polarization to frame and validate an *intrinsically dualistic argument*; second, we would be *seeking to gain something*, therefore sowing the seeds of a new cycle of oppositional suffering; and third, we would be clearly *attempting to solidify* a position that validates self-illusion. In essence, when it comes to the issue of accountability, the bottom line is that *all intent to harm, in all cases and in all circumstances, is an attempt to settle on the part of self-illusion regardless of how it is discursively presented or justified.*

At the same time, in Curflexion, even if there is no clear sense of want and no possibility of actively harming or interfering with others, we have absolutely no control over what other individuals may project in their own confusion and suffering in regards to our actions or motives. In which case, we may be projected and/or accused of being a source of others' pain or suffering as a result of other people's confusion, dualistic perception and wants, as well as their own attempts to solidify their own self-illusion. We definitely cannot control other people's perceptions. If we could, surely the philosophers and sages of the past would have fixed humanity already. So, as long as a dualistic mind manifests on this earth, accusations, conflict and harm will be an expected experience of humans, regardless of whether harm was intended or even truly sustained.

Interestingly enough, as we assimilate and internalize the three paradoxes, our internal perception and experience of harm naturally and gently transforms itself. Through the clarity of Curflexion, when we see harm done, we can now see *genuine confusion*. When we see action without regard for others, we can see an illusory self seeking a settling platform. When we see fear, we can see Being falsely separated as life or death.

In the realm of undifferentiated expression of Being, opposites dissolve, eliminating confusion and the possibility to harm others. Because these opposing positions are no longer necessary to sustain wholesome interaction, Being manifests naturally and effortlessly, given there is nothing to fight for, nothing to defend. Hence, there is no need to take away anything to damage or interfere with others or to attempt to further our attainment or security. With the profound understanding of triparadoxia, we let go of want and therefore, we let go of the attempt to solidify self-illusion.

In Curflexion, the absence of polarization and reification allows for Being to *naturally* emerge as an open, warm, clear, compassionate, flexible, understanding, willing, grounded, direct, courageous and wholesome manifestation of who we truly are. This manifestation is fully sustained by the infinite space of Being and requires no fabrication, no fixing and no sustainment on our part in order for it to manifest freely and harmoniously.

Responsibility

Taking responsibility is not about guilt, shame, retribution, or punishment. Responsibility is about fully surrendering to the moment, allowing the moment to live within completely, and then acting appropriately in each circumstance according to the particulars of the circumstance. Rather than based on a rigid set of rules or projected expectations, we take responsibility fully in every instant regarding everything we are, everything we have been and everything we will be at the same time. There is absolutely no room for evasion and distraction. There is no room for pointing fingers; there is no room for manipulation and interpretation.

When we profoundly welcome Being, we own ourselves in a deeply honest and non-negotiable way. In Curflexion, we take responsibility for our suffering, we take responsibility for our confusion, we take responsibility for our projections and for our faulty interpretation of reality. In the end, we will also take responsibility for moving from contriving form into recognizing limitless space. We take responsibility for our use of language and our internal process of polarization; for our constant attempts to fix the unfixable and for promoting our fragile self-illusion in spite of its endless perils and unsustainable illusory achievements.

We do not take responsibility for having caused the overall condition in which we now find ourselves to be immersed. As discussed early on in this book, we are all innocent of having been brought into this confusing condition. At the same time, we are the only ones who can address and suspend the suffering condition in which we live. We can strive to help others of course and in many cases we will, but we need to remind ourselves that the task of helping others is not an easy one and that each one of us has our own particular road to follow.

Responsibility is unavoidable and self-sustainable simply because there is no way around it, regardless of how much we might try to evade it. The more we try to manipulate and fix our thoughts and emotions, the more we try to evade responsibility, the more powerful these thoughts and emotions will become. It is not until we take full responsibility and completely allow and surrender to what is manifesting within, without defending or buying into it, that these thoughts and emotions end up living the life they need to live after which they simply and gently dissolve into the same space from which they originated.

Socially and personally, we tend to confuse taking responsibility with needing to experience guilt, torment, remorse or shame to show others and ourselves that we have actually taken responsibility. This is seen as a sign of ownership. In reality, guilt, torment, remorse and shame *are simply the result of an unwinnable inner fight* to manipulate what happened or what we now think should have happened or what we think others think should have happened regarding something that has already happened and that is now entirely inaccessible because it will be forever only in the past.

No amount of longing and wishing are going to change what happened; no amount of projection and manipulation can successfully modify the past. Responsibility is not about generating self-inflicted pain for what we have done in the past; rather, it is about stopping the internal fight by truly owning what we did or did not do, what we think we did or think we did not do, as it was, every aspect of it, every moment of it, and resting in this ownership fully and unequivocally, thus allowing Being to manifest through this process.

It is very important to clarify and remind ourselves that we should not understand this form is ownership or responsibility as something that has been forced upon ourselves by other people's interpretation of what we should or should not own. In other words, ownership can only be *owned* from within and not as an imposition from others or the external world. We cannot force ourselves to own something if it does not make sense to us, regardless of how much others would want us to own that same thing. *Ownership is then an internal process of surrender that cannot be falsely produced by imposition from the outside. Ownership originates in the core of our body as we gently acknowledge and allow existence.*

As we do this, we can then act with the clarity and compassion that result from taking full responsibility and ownership of our lives, of our past, of our projections, of our confusion and of all our false internal settlings. This is a clarity and compassion that are not falsified by the expectations of others, by our need for emotional validation, our need to be loved by close relationships, or by a desperate illusory self with a disguised self-serving agenda that hopes to solidify the impossible. Responsibility comes when we stop the internal fight, when we stop defending ourselves from what we falsely believe should not have happened. Responsibility comes as a result of the grounding we experience when we know, without any form of internal argument, that this exquisite reality is all there is, and that as it is, it is complete: nothing lacking, nothing remaining, simply one.

Compassion

Experiencing Being fully and without obstructions seems to be a true and transcendental possibility for us as human beings. This appears to be the original and primordial intuition behind our endless strife and drive towards achievement and success in every possible form – as well as the source of all our suffering and confusion.

The impulse to solve this profound conundrum to allow Being to manifest without being able to address triparadoxia is what fuels our always innocent tendency to hurt ourselves and others. This misunderstood effort to experience Being-As-Is while building a solid self-illusion is the actual driver that propels individuals to do harm. Harm is an assertion of self-illusion. *It is an attempt to internally settle*, regardless of how terrifying, violent, or inconsiderate the impulse may be.

In our confusion, we are all searching for Being. We are seeking the same experience that we all have been desperately looking for. In our confusion we have found ourselves making the mistakes or the promises that in our limited ability, we thought were necessary to experience Being completely. *The profound understanding of this condition is the true meaning, realization and embodiment of compassion.*

Compassion is not the mimicking of rationalized moral axioms at the level of conceptualization and the attempt to practice on a daily basis. Compassion is not the fabricated presentation of ourselves as kind, considerate or selfless. Compassion cannot actually be cultivated or created. Compassion naturally emanates as an effect that comes from understanding. Compassion is a by-product of the profound experiential understanding of triparadoxia in general and in particular of the understanding of the profound implications that come from having countless human beings living in a situation where this entrapped condition seems to be quite common.

As presented in Part 1 of this book, we are innocently caught up in this condition and no one is guilty of it. That is to say that no one is responsible for this entrapment and this delusion. We are confused because of the assumption that our internal world should work with the same rules and causality as the external world and that language is the primordial material that needs to be built in order to internally achieve what we want.

It seems to be common to the human condition that in our profound willingness to search all corners of the earth for our ultimate emancipation and the irreversible incarnation of Being, we seem to be willing to internally settle anywhere and experience all possible human situations in order to achieve our goal, even if sometimes, these goals end up being harmful to ourselves or others. *Unknowingly, in our desperation, our confusion and want, while seeking for Being, we instead actually build a delusory self that ends up keeping us in a consistent form of entrapment promising solid existence.*

The extraordinary good news is that the experience of Curflexion is always available and accessible to us, regardless of our previous personal scorecard. There is no action that could eliminate our chances of accessing Curflexion. *This is the true sense of transcendental forgiveness.* Curflexion is accessible to all regardless of our faults, sins, misunderstandings, guilt, shame, or confusion. Again, this is in no way a justification to harm others because harming others will bring its own internal and profound turmoil. Given that all affirmations and attempts to settle that emanate from self-illusion create immediate and inalienable counter-effects (the experience of non-Being) in an endless cycle that only profound Curflexive silence can restore.

Curflexive silence is a form silence that has little to do with our common understanding of silence. It is a form of silence that is fully active, fully compassionate, fully understanding and fully alive; a form of silence that welcomes all internal and external form, all noise, all confusion and all illusion. A form of silence that grounds and sustains Being before and behind all manifestation.

This extraordinary opportunity should absolutely not be missed. The darkest depths of our accumulated painful narratives are a tremendous burden to carry through life, but the profound understanding of the fact that the way out is always accessible is extraordinary news for us all. This implies that all our possible validation and rumination around any form of deprecatory self-judgment are completely unnecessary, just as all our validation and rumination around purifying darkness from within and saving ourselves from our faults are completely unnecessary as well. The solution, which is the experience of Curflexion, is in neither of these positions, nor any other position that evaluates, compares, differentiates or tries to fix any situation, rather it is precisely in the profound silence (without being necessarily silent) and endless space of Being that reflects itself in Curflexion.

Surrender

When we allow ourselves to exist without polarization and without seeking to solidify illusory ideas of who we think we are, we are allowing Being to manifest in its purest form. Allowing works usually by addressing what is currently appearing in our consciousness-as-mirror in the present moment and *resting in it without reactivity*. In this way we *surrender* to Being as a profound, general and deeply internal disposition towards allowing Being-As-Is to manifest.

Surrender takes an overall view of letting go and hence, resolves self-illusion entirely, offering our life back to the space of the unadulterated energy that fuels everything. By doing so it acknowledges an intelligence that is beyond our conceptual comprehension and beyond our self-serving manipulation.

This is an exquisite path out of confusion. Surrender implies no bargaining. It brings complete trust in the supreme manifestation supporting our existence in every single moment of consciousness. Surrendering is completely empty of gain or loss. We do not surrender by acquiescing to our instincts, to our impulses, to our desires. This is a poor interpretation of surrender. We do not surrender to our intents to settle. We do not surrender to our own enactment of aggression, manipulation, or want. *We can only surrender to what remains after all dualistic conceptualizations resolve. We surrender to emptiness.* Emptiness which again is everything, which again never was and which again has always been the foundation on top of which all illusion manifests.

When we refrain from polarizing our experience through language, when we refrain from trying to buy into oppositional strategies and when we refrain from solidifying self-illusion by not settling anywhere, we are surrendering to Being, In this surrendering we remain open, and in this openness, *we find that we are absolutely complete.* We experience no lack, even if we are alone, even if we have felt incomplete in the past, even if we have wanted company or to live life in a particular way that we have not been able to do. We seek no resolution because there is nothing to be resolved, even if we appear to be lost. We embrace no need of fulfillment, even if we have searched for fulfillment all our lives. We feel no lack – not tomorrow, not in five years, not when we reach some form of liberation. We get there in one instant. The instant we surrender to this instant. *The only instant there is.* Through surrender, the open door is only this particular instant away.

Courage

We can define courage as allowing fear, doubt, tension, stress, anxiety, projection, concern, etc. *to be freely experienced internally on the canvas of our body without getting in the way of what is happening*, without attempting to run from it, fix it, postpone it, tamper with it, validate it, polarize it, manipulate it, change it, solve it, or get rid of it.

This is not what we usually do with our thoughts and emotions of course. When we experience thoughts and emotions that lead to internal discomfort, we generally jump to the rescue of self-illusion and attempt to save it from perceived threat and possible dissolution, or save it from perceived loss of worth. We may then reach out to friends and family, or to our own thoughts of the past, or our ideas and hopes of the future to tighten the experience of who we think we are. We do revisions of what happened, what was said, what we did and we scout the seemingly infinite possible angles that we can use to settle the matter internally in our favor. The experience of allowing and accepting discomfort does not come naturally, given our apparently instinctive (or if not instinctive, then a socially acquired) tendency to attempt to fix our internal experience, which may feel profoundly counterintuitive on many levels to our sense of survival.

Here lies the great challenge when it comes to personal transformation. *Accepting, allowing, welcoming, and surrendering to internal discomfort is the key to internal transformation.* This is a true experience of courage, a true experience of boldness and empowerment.

It is important to notice that accepting and allowing internal discomfort can only happen in the present moment. You may be thinking of something that happened in the past or something that may happen in the future; nevertheless, pain and confusion about these perceived events is always experienced only in the present moment. Courage is an invitation staring at us in every actual instant of discomfort, every second we experience suffering, every moment that we are faced with our greatest fears, doubts and projections. Courage means rising up to the occasion to internally allow, in the form of thoughts and emotions, the apparently unbearable and the seemingly insurmountable its own right to live within our body without interfering.

It is important to remind ourselves that when we courageously allow for our inner experience to live untampered, we are not enhancing it, or validating it, or constructing a bigger edifice out of it. We are not buying into it; we are not solidifying it. On the contrary, when we truly allow any internal thought or emotion with absolutely no expectation of change, these thoughts and emotions just live their lives naturally and gently; and then they softly disappear into thin air, or into the same space they came from originally, with us having to do absolutely nothing except allowing them to live their life.

Imagine that all our thoughts and emotions are like independent beings that enjoy their own life and time on this earth. All of them tend to be very short-lived if we see them in their true present-moment context, even in the worst of times. When these internal entities are tampered with (be it to attempt to make them disappear or to oppose them or to validate and enhance them) and we do not allow them to live their full and unobstructed life, *they will insist in living their life just as they are.* If we oppose them, they will grow bigger, linger and present endless issues and concerns. on the other hand, if we validate or enhance them, they will now require artificial maintenance and upkeep, which results in draining our energy.

We do need to be patient when allowing our internal visitors to freely, neutrally and non-judgmentally live their lives in the canvas of the body, not necessarily because we know these visitors will end up eventually dissolving in space, which will be the case, not because we should try to urge them to move faster or be better, or more efficiently. This intervening approach will only make them stay longer, become stronger and take more of our energy. Full acceptance is full surrender, and *full surrender implies no need to have them go anywhere or even dissolve in the end.*

If we have a persistent or particularly painful internal experience, it will live its life precisely as it needs to be lived and eventually dissolve, exactly at the precise time it would have needed to dissolve - not a second before or after. Courage is in allowing, not in fixing; it is in accepting, not resisting; it is in taking responsibility, not in trying to internally fight or run away. Until this is clear, we will continue to expect something from this process, and as we do this, we will get tangled in a web of expectation and confusion once again.

At first, it will be difficult to open ourselves up to the natural energies that we have been defending from all our lives. We may feel awkward and strange. We may feel vulnerable, afraid, and exposed. *Courage is our raft through these waters.* Allowing, accepting and relaxing into what manifests within is the key to complete surrender and ultimate freedom. Courage will take us there, and when we reach the other shore of every short-lived emotion or thought without trapping them in our own reaction or in our hope of fixing them, we will notice that there is absolutely nothing left of them but pure, endless space, no resistance, no trace, no regret.

If we can do this with most thoughts or emotions that visits causing distress, regardless of their illusory level of risk or threat to self-illusion, then there is absolutely nothing that can get in the way of our realization. There is nothing that can derail us back into engaging with form. *If we can welcome every single internal experience into the canvas of our body and allow it to live its short life freely and openly, all life force within synchronizes with the flow of Being, and we become one with it.* We become one with the flow of the profound manifestation that sustains everything and our sense of separation finally dissolves.

Willingness

When we deeply understand the nature of our human condition and we integrate the reality of the three paradoxes within, we naturally welcome and allow Being-As-Is. Not only that, which in itself is extraordinary considering that we humans tend to live immersed in duality, confusion, and want, defending ourselves from countless imaginary illusions, but in addition to welcoming Being-As-Is, *we also start to be willing and open to whatever the future may bring.* Not because we are seeking to benefit from it, or gain something, or succeed in some imagined situation or condition, or suffer in a particular way, but because *we are simply in love with the whole experience of Being in and of itself.* If we are able to internally allow and welcome everything that is currently happening in our lives as well as everything that has ever happened in the past, then allowing whatever will come in the future becomes a profoundly natural, compassionate and welcomed position, regardless of what this particular future may look like and what it may particularly bring.

Willingness is experienced as a yes to the open and basic invitation of interaction and experience with existence. As a whole, willingness goes beyond polarization, beyond separation, as well as beyond solidification. Willingness is experienced as an open heart, a homecoming song, a soft, kind, and compassionate receipt of the unknown. In essence, willingness is experienced as the unparalleled embodiment of trust in the ever-present and powerful energy that sustains everything.

So, as stated before, when we are willing, we inherently and instantly say yes to the entire phenomenon of life as well as the phenomena that manifests right in front of us every instant. We are present and engaged; there is no defense and no hope for manipulating what is happening. The affirmation of Being is so complete that it actually does not have any possible opposition. In other words, nothing, absolutely nothing else, could be happening except what is actually happening. So, by saying yes immediately and innately to whatever is happening internally, we are then left with the adventure to *actively and compassionately navigate and engage with the implications of that willingness.*

Willingness is not an experience of stupidity or naïveté. It is not the result of lack of awareness or distraction. It is not a consequence of being a doormat or a puppet of someone else or the result of some other form of manipulation. Willingness is not a characteristic of servitude or a process by which we become members of the class of self-proclaimed victimhood. Willingness is not a justification to do or seek harm; it is not a justification to seek confusion or darkness. Willingness is the abode of the *Champions of Being*. It is the space where life is experienced and utilized to its maximum potential. Willingness is the realm of the throbbing hearts, and the awe-inspiring full moons, as well as the breathtaking sunsets. It is the realm of the indescribable and indestructible moments and the exquisite life encounters with the sages and remarkable individuals who transform our lives, until one day, we are able to notice that they were just a reflection of ourselves as a reflexion of ourselves.

Willingness is looking forward to life, to experience, to breath, to being complete. It is looking forward to this instant, and the next, and the next as well as the next, regardless of the arrangement of form, or the condition of our company or circumstance. Willingness is being full on empty, radiant in the dark, in all conditions, and in all situations. It is not needing anything except consciousness-as-mirror in order to be full, contained, engaged and complete just because it is part of the vibrating energy of the universe that constitutes everything that ever was, is and will be. We deeply rest and offer our full trust in life by looking forward to the magnificence of the gift of experience and perception in and of itself, rather than attempting to bargain with the quality of what we experience or perceive. We become the *Welcoming Committee* of life as it manifests.

Action

Early on in this book, readers were warned about the perils of language and the apparent contradictions that can manifest, especially when we are addressing issues and themes such as the ones explored in this book. Action is not an exception to this situation. How can we speak of action if we have stated that there is no such thing as free will and we have seen the profound benefits of surrender? How can we speak of action if there is no one to act? If there is no central self?

Let us explore these questions further. Being-As-Is is not an inert experience; rather, it is an extremely dynamic and action-driven embodiment of life without an illusory self, without internal position or opposition, with profound peace and clarity, and in profound self-sustainment. Curflexive action, as action fully grounded in Being, could be also referred to as Curflexive non-action, in the sense that it is empty of polarization, empty of defense, empty of preference, empty of solidification, and fully grounded in Being.

Curflexive action is non-polarized action, non-dual action and non-settling action, yet there is action, clarity, and purpose at the same time. It is action that manifests in the absence of an illusory self, yet it is action that enjoys the awareness, consciousness and vitality of Being as the wholesome ground of experience. It is action that springs from Curflexive silence, manifests through Curflexive silence and rests in Curflexive silence, while it is complete, sustained, and congruent.

Curflexive action is completely absent of doubt and it is fully self-reliable. It is not constructed and sustained with rationalization or dualization. It is action that is complete every instant, where nothing is lacking and nothing is expected, yet it does not settle, it does not drive a purpose at the same time, and it is not necessarily experienced in a defined and particular way. Curflexive action allows the world to manifest as we surf the waves of reality with grace, enthusiasm, clarity and delight.

It is important to note that Curflexive action may not necessarily appear to be adequate to other people around us. There is no such thing as perfection in the general eye of the beholder, given that every single one of us has a very particular recipe constituting self-illusion. Also, it is very important not to confuse Curflexive action with all-pleasing action; these are definitely not the same thing. Given that we humans generally live in a world of confusion, internal language, judgment, separation, dualization and solidification, it is naturally and intrinsically impossible for us to constantly please others. Rather than this having a negative connotation, this condition actually brings a profoundly liberating understanding.

Pleasing others is clearly impossible because the pleasing or non-pleasing of others is only a result of someone else's self-illusion position and never the result of what we do or end up not doing, let alone the true experience of Being-As-Is. Acceptance or rejection comes from others, independent of whatever we do or do not do. People accept or reject something based on their own manifestation of their self-illusion and not on the actual action we undertook in hopes of being accepted or rejected.

Considering that it is inherently impossible to consistently please others, we need to ask ourselves, "How much time do we spend trying to do this?" Trying to convince others of our worth? Trying to be likeable? Trying to appear interesting, intelligent, loveable, committed, or even ambitious, aggressive, difficult or assertive if needed? How much time do we invest in what others may be thinking of us, of what we do, or what we fail to do, or of what we think or fail to think, or of what we feel or fail to feel?

Curflexive action is necessarily an experience validated internally and not through the reference of others' self-illusion. It is very important not to understand internal as subjective, invalid, fragile or inconsistent, irrational or harmful for others. On the contrary, in the case of Curflexive action (i.e., action that springs out of the firm realization of triparadoxia), we can definitely say that internal refers to *an inalienable, sustained, incorruptible, grounded, compassionate, humble, and peaceful understanding,* where no doubt manifests, yet full action is sustained neutrally and effortlessly.

How do we actually do this? How do we experience action without an illusory self? By connecting to and allowing for Being-As-Is to manifest through us. By letting go of everything and still noticing that we do not drop to the ground inert, but remain, silent, focused, alert, complete, welcoming, and flexible. How do we keep on going? How do we plan our next steps? We do not need to plan through self-illusion. We only need to embody triparadoxia to a level where Being simply flows naturally as a result of profound experiential understanding of the fact that (a) language and polarization cannot truly encompass Being; (b) the fact that when we summon the good, we also summon the bad as part of a continuous cycle; and (c) the fact that there is no central, hegemonic me running the show inside our hearts and minds.

When I say connecting to and allowing for Being-As-Is, I am referring to opening up for action to come from the realm of Curflexive silence that exists behind who we think we are, which is a space of neutral emanation where there are no dualities, where we innately see things more clearly. This happens spontaneously, openly, fluidly, and without an internal conversation, strategy, or expectation. It happens when we are internally present, when we are internally undivided, when we are internally whole and we act and speak from where there is no polarization driving a need to settle: in other words, from our true, grounded and direct experience and profound understanding of Being, whatever this may be at the time of the interaction.

Being has a form of innate intelligence in the same way a parent would instinctively protect a child from harm. There is no language, conceptualization, or solidification going on as part of this process. In a similar way, but at an entirely different level, and far beyond instinctive reactions, **Being knows how to decide, react, surrender, allow, or engage in absolutely every single situation with complete grounding, integrity, compassion, and self-sustainment.** Decision making in this case of openness turns out to be one of the most joyous experiences we can have when we are in the flow of Being, entirely eliminating the uncertainty, the coming and going, the doubt, the anxiety and the second-guessing that come from deciding at the level of self-illusion.

Interestingly enough, the moment we speculate as to what would this look like, or what would this be, what would happen in which situation, and with whom, we would be falling back into the realm of self-illusion, and we would be losing our direct experience of reality. We would now be planning, strategizing and imagining what Curflexive action would look like or be like in particular situations or under certain conditions, which again would deliver us into the realm of dualization.

It is very important to know that in some cases, self-illusion may *falsely* present itself as Being and *pretend* that all kinds of settling platforms (thoughts, concepts, emotions, and actions) *are actually coming from Being itself.* In this case, we should surely expect considerable suffering to follow, given that sooner or later, the montage will dissolve (as it always happens) and we will be left with the pain of having settled in these illusory platforms as well as with the internal confusion resulting from it.

In essence, self-illusion, in and of itself, cannot sustain an integral and grounded decision. It cannot sustain it because it is indeed an illusion, reacting to illusions, while trying to hopelessly solidify its own delusory experience. In this case, whatever self-illusion decides will be decided through settling in some platform that will certainly eventually dissolve, and we will definitely face the painful consequences that come from this dissolution.

Trusting and fully surrendering to the complete capacity of Being may take some time. Self-illusion will always present clear doubts about this strategy. At the same time, we can also easily notice that things come out to be wrong, *even when we invest countless days or years on thinking them through at the level of self-illusion.* Therefore, polarization, rationalization, conceptualization, and dualization certainly do not guarantee adequate action.

Being-As-Is is an engaging, non-discursive experience that manifests beyond dualistic entrapments and is naturally compassionate and understanding of the complexities presented by self-illusion, given that it supersedes it and contains it at the same time. As the delusory nature of self-illusion resolves, *Being-As-Is manifests without losing experiential understanding of the illusory entrapment we have been exposed to,* and that so many continue to be exposed to. *We are not blind-sighted or short sighted by the experience of flow that comes with Curflexion.* Validating or justifying aggression, violence, breaking the rules, or ill will through embodying Being is, in itself, a manipulation of self-illusion cleverly disguising itself once again.

Curflexive action is based in the most inalienable triparadoxial understanding that we may embody. It is the cornerstone of our profound internal truth as action. *Curflexive action is sustained by compassion and understanding naturally and not as a result of a personal strategy to enact compassion, but rather as a natural emanation coming from the profound experiential understanding of triparadoxia.* Illusion naturally dissolves and compassion naturally arises as a result of this profound understanding. If we act from our deepest understanding of the three paradoxes and engage with others and the world actively, deeply, and honestly in the present moment and without any rigid future strategies or past baggage, from the space that we know without a doubt is our true human condition, then life manifests in perpetual flow, containment, fulfillment, peace and perfect understanding.

In this case, there is grounded, contained and sustained action with no second thoughts, no doubt, no hope, no want, and no waiting for something different to happen. We allow for silence, for stability, and for presence. We engage as complete human beings and not as incomplete seekers of what we do not have and will never be able to have.

When we are having a conversation with someone else in profound understanding of triparadoxia, *Being-As-Is shines through.* The language we are using is flexible and inclusive; our experience of opposites is neutral; the solidification of ourselves, others, society and the human condition is simply not there. Communicating and interacting with others from the profound empirical understanding of triparadoxia situates ourselves in a unique space of dynamism, enjoyment, interaction, and fulfillment that is inaccessible to us from the dimension of self-illusion.

Curflexion

In the analogy of the two reflecting mirrors, the possibility of considering that we could be one of the mirrors was presented. Our consciousness-as-mirror actually serves that exact same purpose. There is nothing we can be conscious of that is not presented to that consciousness-as-mirror. This includes objects of the material world as well as thoughts, ideas, dreams, and or all other kinds of physical, mental, emotional, or spiritual experiences.

The question that begs to be asked now of course is: "If I am one of the two mirrors, who or what is the other mirror?" If we need another mirror, we would be falling again into the trap of *two* and, therefore, the trap of seeking and differentiation. So moving deeper into the analogy of Curflexion, we need to consider that in reality, *there is actually no second mirror*, but rather only one consciousness-as-mirror reflecting **itself on itself** as a **curved reflection**, instead of some other external or internal reflective surface. *Therefore, when consciousness-as-mirror looks for itself and* *moves beyond (or remains before) language, dualistic separation and illusory self, it finds itself again as consciousness-as-mirror actually manifesting Curflexion as reflexion of its endless reflection.*

Curflexion is naturally accessed as the game of distraction and solidification resolves through a process of honest and profound inquiry into the true nature of our human condition. At times, this only happens momentarily, especially when we are starting to question the apparently unquestionable. Sometimes, suddenly, the cocoon of self-illusion cracks open to resolve entirely and be no more, allowing our energy to experience life as complete Being-As-Is, which is again part of everything that is and exists without differentiation, without subject and object.

Most of us have had some form of Curflexive-intuitive experience at some point or other in our lives. Overall, these experiences have a profound effect on us. In most cases, they serve as reliable markers for our inner exploration and generally have profound implications in our lives. Unfortunately, many individuals who end up having these experiences, for one reason or another, tend to try to replicate these by doing something or trying to oppose something internally to get there, instead of just allowing without action; hence, they get trapped in the same cycle they are trying to escape from.

The realm beyond conceptual form is as real as anything else in our experience, while not communicable at the same time. *All expression of its magnificence, simplicity,* and completeness is tampered with and diluted by the heaviness of polarization and language. Yet, this tampering and dilution do not mean that the realm is nonexistent; it simply requires to be fully lived in complete surrender, connection and spontaneity. If we allow our internal edifice to soften or be resolved so that we open up to the intuition that comes from within, we will allow ourselves to experience sudden glimpses into the nature of Curflexion. These glimpses will become stronger as the understanding will become deeper, allowing for spells of clarity and insight that go beyond and above any descriptive or narrative embodiment of Being, eventually resolving self-illusion and manifesting as Being-As-Is.

Deconstructing the three paradoxical conditions through honest and profound inquiry leads to sustained liberation. This is the door into Curflexion. We let go and liberate ourselves precisely because we understand triparadoxia at a deep experiential level and not because we actually practice or do anything in order to let go. We surrender because we understand triparadoxia and not because we practice surrender, and we allow Being-As-Is because we understand triparadoxia and not because we practice Being-As-Is or because we finally find a way to fix, settle, or sustain self-illusion.

Experience beyond language, polarization, attachment, aversion, and solidification of a central self is the source of all transcendental, mystical, or spiritual experiences. It is also the source of an endless flow of peace, joy, compassion and connectedness that is beyond description or categorization. This reality *cannot be expressed because it is the inexpressible, and it cannot be contained in any form of thought because it is the inconceivable, yet it fuels everything and it embodies everyone.* The true question at this point is not whether we can describe this space or if it is describable at all. The true question at this point is whether human experience is viable or even possible in a realm completely absent of solidified polarization.

In reality, life beyond polarization, categorization and solidification of a central self is completely viable. An endless number of peers in this voyage of life seem to have experienced this non-dual phenomenon in all cultures and throughout all times. It has been given many names and conceived in many different ways for the purposes of communicating its relevance to others. This could serve as evidence, even if we have not yet experienced such liberated space.

Poetry and prayer written throughout the history of humankind from all corners of the earth also clearly point to the non-dual experience. We have countless accounts of individuals who have allowed Being-As-Is to manifest through letting go of their self-illusion. More importantly, and moving away from history and other people's experiences, it is easy to see that we all carry the intuition of Curflexion within: in our daily strife, in our constant want, in our endless attempt to oppose our internal experience, in our chase for love, in our eagerness to feel complete and in our persistent longing for what we do not have. Somehow, we know it is there, behind all the noise and behind all the distraction. This intuition is our most precious gift while in the dark and cold cave of confusion and shadows.

Curflexion is embodied by allowing for our reflection to manifest *from* the space of our own reflection as only one mythical mirror reflecting on itself. It is accessed by allowing consciousness-as-mirror *from* the space of consciousness-as-mirror, by allowing for the origin of Being *from* the origin of Being, only to find the Infinite reflected as complete internal freedom, regardless of our circumstance. This is the perfect space where action, understanding, connection and sustainment manifest.

5

Integration

There is a vessel that travels lightly
between the two shores,
supported by an ever-silent wind
that replaces all words.

Unreached by thought, concept, hope,
nor will, projection, or want,
the new lands become alive only
when we pay the price in living gold!

Every ounce of illusory self shall be the offer.
Every song of want will be exhausted.
Every two will become one
resolving every difference into thin air.

It is done!

Practice

As mentioned several times throughout the book, our internal condition cannot be fixed, or patched, or ameliorated by using the causal mechanisms we use in our daily lives to fix issues in our external or mechanical world, such as zooming into a problem and injecting the proverbial antidote or anti-cause. *We achieve Curflexion through the profound, experiential understanding of triparadoxia;* through deeply realizing the impossibility to achieve the unachievable at three levels: (a) we cannot fully reduce the experience of Being to words and dualities (The Language Paradox); (b) every time we buy into any solution or try to fix our internal suffering, we are at the same time buying into promoting and securing future suffering of the same nature (The 2-for-1 Paradox); and finally (c) self-illusion does not really exist, hence, it is only a delusion that cannot be sustained through any platform (Nowhere to Settle Paradox).

To deeply experience and integrate these paradoxes, I will present several approximations in this following section that will allow for us to empirically explore the nature of Being-As-Is, in order to embody what is actually there and not what we have socially, mentally and emotionally constructed throughout our lives, which has kept us confined, alone, and incomplete.

Curflexion cannot be produced by *actively* allowing or surrendering to an experience. *Allowing, letting go and surrendering to something will never be achieved by actively doing anything.* Action only brings more action in return (i.e., reaction), hence not the true experience of allowing, letting go and surrendering that comes naturally and effortlessly from understanding. *When we understand through honest, experiential exploration, we release naturally, we allow, let go and surrender without any effort, without any drive, without any want, without any hidden agenda, without any directive, without any goal.*

From the time we are born, most of us are socialized to buy into the concept of achieving something great. Yes, it is usually something great in reference to our starting point. For a life in the slums, it may be the ability to graduate from elementary school; for a sailor, it could be to sail around the world; and to a musician, it could be to earn enough money to survive while playing on the street.

Conditioning towards achievement or status is very common and comes with an equally difficult side of lack and separation. If achieving something other than what we are in this moment and time is so important, it necessarily means that who we are now is not ok, complete or worthy of being as it is, which is simply and plainly impossible for Being-As-Is. Furthermore, achievement is usually defined as something extraordinary in reference to the starting point. Therefore, by its own definition it is highly unlikely to be accomplished. Considering that we are all human, and we all suffer, and we are all trapped in the complications of language and dualistic confusion, is it probable that most of us would not be able to achieve the already unlikely goal that we have projected onto ourselves. Therefore, *Curflexion is not about achievement. It is not about finding the new positive to debunk the old negative. It is not about accumulating merit or practice or knowledge or status. Curflexion is about embodying absolutely everything we need to be complete in this precise moment.*

The exploration of triparadoxia does not require a special setting, ambience or any form of manicured circumstances. It does not require a secret meditation or breathing technique, and it certainly does not require blind following or the assumption of any unquestioned premise. Your personal understanding, as well as the full ownership of your experience, are the foundation stones on the quest for transformation. We also do not need to necessarily change our lives, live in seclusion or in some form of specific environment, or give up family life or our work. Modifying these things for the purposes of achieving Curflexion will only develop a conceptual construct that will complicate things even more, given that we would now be engaged in a process of achieving something rather than allowing. Curflexion will never manifest as a result of constructing, fixing, or strategizing anything; the more we use this approach in our life to try to access Curflexion, the further away from Curflexion we will end up.

It is important to reiterate that in all instances, these practices should only be used when addressing our internal experience for the purposes of self discovery and personal inquiry. If you are in a situation where you need medical attention, where your safety is at stake, where communication is required, or any other situation that would call for attention, you should seek this attention accordingly. In all cases, for all practices presented in this book, you remain wholly responsible for your understanding, your experience and your actions.

All practices presented here are non-progressive ones. By this, I mean that these are approximations where we should not expect the development of a particular sequential experience. There is no particular goal that we should look for, but rather, a generally immediate and accessible result of the embodiment of Curflexion through deep experiential understanding. It may take some time to assimilate these approximations correctly, it may also take some time for the understanding of the three paradoxes to root deeply in our hearts and naturally dissolve the confusion, tension, suffering, and misunderstandings that we have been subject to for so long, but this does not mean that one should train for many years with an objective-driven mind.

These practices are nothing more than suggestive in and of themselves. These are not prescribed practices, but only approximations that seem to come naturally from the understanding of triparadoxia. Some of the practices I will share in this book have been the result of my own direct personal experience. Other practices presented in this book are adaptations of practices coming from a rich and centuries long tradition of non-dual philosophy, particularly from the Advaita School. Please feel free to devise your own practices. As you integrate and embody the triparadoxial understanding of Curflexion, you may see particular approaches that may be of specific benefit to you and may look different than what is being suggested in that section of the book.

Curflexion is a present-moment understanding of our internal condition and only relevant in the present moment, which is actually the only and everlasting moment there is. We should not buy into any progression and let go of any sense of achievement, expectation, or realization. Full allowing implies even letting go of solving suffering or having something eventually change as a result of our engagement. The objective is only to engage in the understanding of the moment, without an illusion, without expectation, without a sense of future culmination or success. Some may perceive that the experience of Curflexion deepens as time goes by and as we explore and become familiar with the phenomenon. This experience is not the result of a methodological process, but rather of the understanding of triparadoxia and Being-As-Is. You should also not expect any form of exalted state of mind other than what is present for you right here, right now, in every moment you live.

Noticing

Any internal situation, thought, emotion, or experience can be examined through the lens of the three paradoxes, with unique and sometimes immediate results. However, to do so, we need to initially identify what is actually happening in the moment in our consciousness-as-mirror without over analyzing it – just noticing. This may seem like a pretty straightforward process; nevertheless, it may be quite difficult at first and sometimes tricky, even after we become experienced in doing so.

Distraction is so pervasive in our cultural context and surroundings that we often fail to notice how our thoughts and emotions compound concepts that then produce innate impulses, which we have wired in through socialization or conditional behavior, and all of this without us really noticing what actually happened. Being able to notice what we are internally experiencing in the form of thoughts, emotions, polarizations, concepts and feelings in the present moment is a basic step towards being able to deconstruct suffering.

There is a fine line though between being aware of a thought, emotion, and evaluation and being overly aware, tense, or stressed about being aware; understanding awareness and the nature of awareness is very important. Noticing what is going on internally, while fully allowing, without trying to control it or without stressing about it, is our basic approach to internal examination and the actual door to our much-needed triparadoxial understanding.

If we over analyze what we notice inside of us, we actually give it more weight. As it appears more solid to us, it becomes more real as well; hence, noticing should be understood as simply noticing, in a similar way as we notice a car driving by or being simply and gently attentive of people we do not know crossing the street. It is perceiving what manifests, while interacting with it in *neutral awareness*.

It is important to know that noticing is not an aim in itself. Nothing happens by just noticing. Noticing is an initial step to understanding how we tend to misunderstand reality. *When we are able to neutrally notice our internal world, we are then able to inquire into the nature of the three paradoxes within the particular experience we are having.* When we are caught up in what we are noticing, then there is no space for inquiry and no space for understanding. Of course, it is sometimes difficult to see our internal experience in a neutral way. As we notice and inquire into what we perceive and we allow for the triparadoxial understanding to infuse our inquiry, we can also then begin to allow for neutrality to manifest.

When we start noticing, it is normal to sometimes become overwhelmed with what is going on inside. At first, all that appears inside may seem relevant, important, unique, or crucial. Things that before would mostly have slid by unnoticed may now seem overwhelming and even heart wrenching. It is just a matter of allowing and welcoming our internal experience without any expectation of gain, change, or resolution. In this way, the intensity of our perception will adjust to a point where we notice what is actually going on inside, to a point where we can begin our internal triparadoxial exploration without being overwhelmed.

Everything is up for examination: stressful internal events, hopeful internal events, and painful internal events as well as pleasurable internal events. We do not seek to keep the joyful events and only examine the hurting ones. This is a fast way into the chamber of duality once more. All possible internal events should be investigated under the light of the three paradoxes, without any hope or expectation of achieving clarity at the same time. We simply allow for the visiting distractions to naturally live whatever life they need to live until they dissolve in the canvas of our body. We also do not seek to replace these with anything else. We must be careful, though, because even "dissolution" as a goal would take us right back into the objective-driven mind again, which would then solidify self-illusion into trying to achieve a particular resolution, then buying into the counter-goal at the same time and starting the cycle of dissatisfaction all over again.

Noticing is a dispassionate and detached endeavor that yet requires our full attention. This attentive letting go may be somewhat counter-intuitive as well. We may think that what usually requires our attention would be something we would naturally tend to want to control, inspect, dissect, guide or direct. In this case, noticing would be more of a combination of deep attentiveness with a profound expression of understanding that allows everything that appears in our consciousness-as-mirror to manifest freely in the canvas of our mind and body.

Journeying

This is an individual journey. From time immemorial, we have eagerly entertained the well-intended fantasy that we can change others. This feeling and internal experience is simply another kind, yet misleading, misconception aimed at building, sustaining and solidifying self-illusion. This misconception is incredibly powerful, one whose implications have a tremendous affect on our lives and the lives of others. This is where we get the enormously powerful drive to fix our travel companions, our partner, our group or our community. Yet, as we attempt to change others, we are clearly missing something at the core.

As we have said before, in relationships, we seek others to confirm our existence. We need others to *see* us, to acknowledge us and to validate self-illusion, our ideas, our concepts and what we are all about: our passions, our reasons to be alive. We need others to validate the illusory idea that we can liberate others. Of course, unfortunately, and no matter how hard we try, we will tend to be disappointed only to constantly end up feeling incapable, incomplete, unnoticed, disrespected, unmet, and alone again.

As human beings, we seem to feel innately separated from something intrinsically welcoming, originally complete, unconditional, all-sustaining, all-allowing and absolute. In reality, what is happening is that we simply feel separated from Being. We precisely feel separated because we are, actually, somehow, perceptionally separated from Being as a result of the completely unnecessary and innocent creation and sustainment of an illusory self. The way back to Being can only be travelled within each of us, and by definition, it would be clearly impossible to do this work for someone else. It would also be impossible to have someone else do it for us, or even for us to have others do their work for themselves given the unique constitution of each of our illusory selves.

Self-illusion only gets resolved from the inside out, particularly when perceived through the profound experiential understanding of triparadoxia. Most attempts toward liberation coming from the outside, coming from others, will generally be considered as some form of intrusion as well as some form of illusory construction, unless the individual is completely open and willing to resolve the illusion through their own unwavering surrender.

We can always share our path with others or make ourselves familiar with the paths of others. We can read books, ancient or recent, or listen to current self-experience and narrative. We can form part of a group of people interested in sharing their experience. We can sincerely and profoundly appreciate the experiences of previously resolved self-illusions or the wonders of particular manifestations and expressions of Being-As-Is. We can follow the writings, comments, suggestions and recommendations of others. Of course, we can also seek similar-minded individuals to share some part of the experience. Nevertheless, we must each travel our own inner labyrinths, which of course look unlike anything else we have actually heard of or been shown in the past because each of us has our own particular concoction in the brew of internal confusion.

Once we experience our own grounded and profound understanding of triparadoxia and begin to live our true experience of Being, we can then easily and quickly identify Being-As-Is naturally when it is narrated, presented, or experienced by others. In this situation, when we read or hear of the pure expression of pristine and clear consciousness-as-mirror reflected in and of itself, it is not only immediately recognizable, but profoundly understandable with its myriad of personal differences, attenuations, temporal marks, and particularities. The language of Being becomes exquisitely transparent, and the horizon becomes clear and all encompassing. We can then see the different manifestations of Being that are trying to be funneled and expressed through the countless limitations of language and dualization. Now, we can finally develop an exquisite, all-inclusive perspective of Being as something told or narrated. Only from Being can we actually recognize Being as reflected in language and polarizations, but not the other way around.

6

Practices

Do without a doer.
Exist without defense.
Achieve by allowing.

Cleaning the house of everlasting space
we become everything!

Allowing and welcoming
without any action, hope or want
is the new path.
The path of no path.

In the mornings, allow.
In the afternoons, welcome.
In the evenings, let go.

Be the stage of
everlasting presence!

Canvas

Accepting is fully allowing and welcoming whatever manifests internally in our consciousness-as-mirror without getting in its way, without fighting it, without validating it, without polarizing it, without fixing it and without engaging in any form of transactional or transformational process. It is to fully allow and connect with any internal experience without interpretation, without defense, without validation. It is to fully relax into every possible situation with an empty mind (Dowman, 2013). In this way we reverently allow any internal experience *the right to live and manifest that all other forms in existence enjoy through Being.*

This is an act of equilibrium, fairness, and honoring Being-As-Is. When we fight, resist, or interpret whatever manifests internally in our consciousness-as-mirror, we are building a barrier to life and to the energy that fuels everything. We are separating ourselves from our source of clarity, joy, compassion, understanding and freedom, and we are resorting to hopelessly living only on crumbles and hints of Being-As-Is.

Allowing an internal emotional experience to freely live in the canvas of our body does not mean that we are validating what we are experiencing as true or as real or as grounds for any justifiable action. *We allow negative internal emotional experiences to live in the all-welcoming canvas of our body because this is a path towards their dissolution and our freedom.* As we allow their existence, this energy will actually *burn itself out on its own.* It is important to remind ourselves that any settling, validation, and dualized interpretation towards action will result in more confusion and pain.

In practice, when we identify a particular negative thought or emotion manifesting internally, be it from our past, present, or future, we can begin by inviting this thought or emotion into the all-welcoming canvas of our body. As we invite this internal experience into our body, we allow for it to live its life without any obstruction or interpretation. We allow for the canvas of our body to welcome and hold any internal experience openly and freely. We welcome it without wanting anything different, without taking any action around it, without validating it, without wanting it to change, or without wanting to get any particular results from it. None whatsoever. Instead, we accept, by allowing all possible expressions of this sensation (or any other sensation whatsoever) to freely live the entirety of its life in the canvas of our body, without opposition and without buying into it. We do this to the point where we end up actually accepting and appreciating whatever manifests internally as we see it appear, live and dissolve, regardless of how menacing it may appear to self-illusion and without any form of interpretation.

Once again, if you are in a situation that requires action rather than contemplation, I trust that you will address the situation accordingly. As much as language and polarization may be poor vehicles to sustain the vastness of Being, they are still our most effective tools when it comes to communication, survival, interaction and safety.

As we allow and accept any internal form or sensation that we might have considered negative, it will now be experienced as pure Being and welcomed as such. This approximation has the incredible gift of liberating all kinds of apparently terrible internal experiences. *When we truly know that fear, guilt, loss, and all other manifestations of self-illusion are only opposed and labeled neutral energy, the edifice or separation dissolves.*

Triparadoxia

*I*nquiring *into what internally manifests in our awareness through the scrutiny of the three paradoxes is the main door into Curflexion.* Deepening the understanding of the paradoxes through examination of our inner experience in the present moment without expectation of attainment opens up the door to Being-As-Is.

Knowing that language and dualization attempt the impossible, by trying to divide our internal experiences into the adequate and inadequate camps, allows for the space necessary to bring Being to manifest. Understanding that buying into a solution implies instantly buying into its opposite prevents us from investing our energy into an already lost endeavor. Being deeply aware that self-illusion is non-existent and therefore, has nowhere to settle, nowhere to be built, and nowhere to hide, simply because it is a constructed illusion, allows for the experience of ultimate welcoming and surrender.

1. What would this internal experience be without language and polarization?

This first question will allow us to deeply explore the Language Paradox. You can begin by identifying any stressful, unpleasant or negative internal event, emotion or thought in your consciousness-as-mirror, and invite this experience to move into the canvas of your body. *While in the canvas of your body, explore what that negative internal experience would be without language and polarization.* Notice and examine this proposal deeply. As you do this, remain in that same space of internal exploration and, when needed, come back to the question: *"What would this internal experience be without language and polarization?"* Then again notice, breathe and allow for space and understanding to manifest.

2. What would this internal experience be without trying to fix it or solve it?

This second question will guide us through the internal exploration of the 2-for-1 Paradox. Again, identify any possible stressful or negative internal experience in your consciousness-as-mirror and invite this experience to move into the canvas of your body. *While in the canvas of your body ask yourself: "What would this internal experience be without trying to fix it or solve it?"* Simply allowing and breathing as you inquire and examine this question in the present moment without expecting the internal experience to change, without indeed trying to fix it, without trying for it to go away, without trying to validate it, without trying for it to stay. You simply notice, allow, breathe and inquire.

3. What would this internal experience be without needing to settle anywhere or needing to be anyone?

This third question will guide us through the exploration of the Nowhere to Settle Paradox. Again, identify any possible internal negative or stressful experience in your conscious-ness-as-mirror and invite this experience to move into the canvas of your body. *While in the canvas of your body ask yourself, "What would this internal experience be without having to settle anywhere or having to be anyone?"* In other words, without trying to define who you are, what you are about, what your passion is, or what is your purpose in life in reference to the experience you are having. In the same way, you can also support this exploration by noticing, al-lowing, and breathing consistently through your inquiry. We do this while holding the space of direct experiential openness and understanding, without language, without dualization, without evaluation, and without expectation – simply allowing Being to manifest internally.

Overall, the way to approximate these questions should be as a profound exploration into our indefinable inner experience. *These questions are not an invitation to start a conversation with self-illusion.* These questions are not part of a strategy and we do not seek any form of validation through them. *For each of these questions, we are actually not looking for a conceptual answer; we are not looking for a solution.* Rather, *we are allowing for the all-sustaining space that supports them to manifest.*

As stated before, all thoughts, emotions and perceptions are up for examination: positive, negative, and neutral, as well as all levels in between. It is generally viable to start with stressful internal events because they are easier to identify and address, nevertheless, we can further use the canvas of our body, or the lens of triparadoxia, to explore the space behind self-illusion and dualistic perception for any internal event appearing in our consciousness-as-mirror.

Evidently, we need to be mindful not to apply these questions in practical situations where organization, communication, interaction, survival or safety are at stake. These questions are also not applicable to the realm of traditional conceptual knowledge. Also, if you are experiencing any situation where you need to use language to ask for help, or if you have to fix a situation in which you feel you are being mistreated, or if you have a need to assert yourself for safety reasons, you should certainly do so, when needed and as needed. These questions are intended to be instruments of exploration into the profound nature of our essential reality.

In the end, how would we know we have arrived to the space beyond the questions? Well, when we are there, there is clear certainty of Being. There is clarity, peace, and understanding of the nature of our existence, yet it is quite profound and silent, without an overt concept. *Certainty of Being is not constructed, not achieved and not reached through any thought process, any system, or any effort. It is an innate result of profound understanding, without duality and without solidification.*

Reflecting endless space through looking at what is behind the noise from behind the noise, at what is behind the confusion from behind the confusion, and what is behind the distraction from behind the distraction leads to finding our same awareness reflecting at our own awareness in a perfect circle of self-sustainment. Living a life where experience becomes the constant enjoyment of whatever manifests, without expecting anything different than what manifests, permits for the flow that gives ultimate understanding to our lives. It is arriving at the space we know we were born to arrive at. It is reaching our destination without any progression, effort, or direction. It is Being boundless. It is Being complete.

Signposts

In the realm of Being, suffering naturally resolves. When we suffer, we tend to look for a way to interact with that same suffering and with whatever we believe is causing it so that we may somehow be free of it. We generally engage in looking for a solution or in other cases, we engage with the suffering by validating it; thereby defending and solidifying the complications we perceive ourselves to be facing as well as our own roles in them.

When we solidify the experience of form that we are naturally exposed to in this life through our thoughts or emotions, we are caught fighting a battle with illusory shadows and therefore, there is not much to hold on to. Our thoughts and emotions are incredibly fluid and changeable and self-illusion is tremendously slippery and very difficult to focus on. Nevertheless, there is something that is systematically consistent that functions as a signpost that can serve us well in our experience towards profound inner peace. *This signpost is actually our own suffering —*

our own internal pain. In a nutshell, suffering is the effect of an internal misalignment, the effect of an internal separation. We suffer because we perceive we are missing something – some part of the puzzle of the understanding of the nature of our reality. *We suffer because, in essence, we are internally resisting something* and we are resisting something not because we are bad or defective. We are resisting something because we want whatever is happening to be different than what is happening, which, as we now well know, is a complete lost cause.

Suffering as a signpost can be extraordinarily helpful if we use it as a call for attention, rather than solidifying the perception that it needs to be fixed. Therefore, we can use suffering as a signpost to notice what we are missing or what we are not seeing in this moment, rather than buying into the thought or emotion and taking it as a real situation or a real threat. When we deeply understand triparadoxia, suffering resolves on its own accord. When we suffer, we know that we are missing something in our understanding, so we can learn to use our suffering as a door to move away from suffering, rather than using our suffering as the entrance hall into more suffering.

In this case, our body serves as an extraordinary vehicle for emancipation. Our body becomes the gauge of our confusion. It shows us, through its own levels of stress, anxiety and overall discomfort, how much we are misaligned. Therefore, it is a signal of our internal separation. When we notice stress, anxiety, resistance or internal pain, we could simply stop for a second and deeply ask ourselves *"What am I missing?"* or *"What am I not seeing?"* and then engage in an honest and profound process of triparadoxial exploration.

It is important to remember here that any way of attempting to manipulate our thoughts or emotions will backfire. All justification, validation, polarization, or solidification will not work. We do not ask, "What am I missing" to then self-justify an internal story about how it is that I am right and the other person is wrong. A distinct characteristic of Curflexion is that we are at peace with whatever manifests and there is no need to polarize our experience. Polarization requires that we invest energy in the actual positioning, maintaining and sustaining of whatever we are believing, always backfiring in the end, throwing us back into the pool of pain as we well know by now.

So when we ask, "What am I missing?" or "What am I not seeing?" we ask from a space of genuine inquiry into the three paradoxes and not looking for validation and support on the side of our internal opposing forces in the form of concepts, thoughts, emotions, or rational strategies. It is a call for understanding rather than a call for battle; it is a call for allowing rather than a call to prove something. When we notice tension and stress in our body, we are actually being invited to open up and explore triparadoxia, instead of instinctively hunkering down and preparing for internal or external dispute.

When we notice the signpost of tension, emotional pain, or stress in our body, we can invite these internal experiences into the canvas of our body and ask ourselves the three triparadoxial questions: (a) What would this internal experience be without language and polarization? (b) What would this internal experience be without trying to fix it or solve it? and (c) what would this internal experience be without trying to settle anywhere or be anyone?

As we allow our inquiry to embody the understanding of the nature of our reality, we will notice that tension dissolves, stress evaporates, and that we remain flexible, open, and connected with life. This experience may not be easy at first because we are actually wired to react to our internal discomfort, rather than to allow it. As the experience of Curflexion deepens and stabilizes, we can see clear results when using our own suffering as a signpost into clarity and understanding.

No Option

Profound understanding of triparadoxia allows for Being to manifest through the natural and compassionate letting go of language, dualities, and the solidity of a central self. When we let go of these three constructions, we will naturally be unable to find validation for self-illusion. *When we let go of the search to validate self-illusion, our wanting mind collapses into original sustaining, neutral, and boundless energy.* It surrenders folding into the space that was behind it all along. It self-identifies and becomes one with the vastness behind every concept, behind every justification, behind every polarization and behind every rationalization.

When we gain direct and profound understanding of our paradoxical condition by not falling into the traps of separation, achievement, and sustainment, we are actually saying no to everything that we thought would lead to the final settling and solidification of self-illusion. In essence, we are saying no to the building blocks of self-illusion. In this way, we end up fully letting go while remaining complete, here, breathing, now.

One of the most direct ways to access Curflexion, as it has been practiced for centuries in the Advaita tradition of non-dual philosophy, is when we engage in a process of gently and non-defensively responding *"not this"* to everything that manifests in consciousness-as-mirror. By saying "not this" to all possible expressions of our dualistic mind, we are simply meaning: *"This is not Being."* Anything and everything that manifests in consciousness-as-mirror that is not the actual pure and empty reflexion of consciousness-as-mirror itself is inherently a diversion and a distraction from Being-As-Is and, therefore, the door to internal separation and dualization.

For example, if we find that we have the internal experience of fear manifesting within for whatever possible reason (e.g., fear of death, loneliness, shame, ridicule, failure, etc.) and we gently and kindly say to ourselves, *"No, this is not Being"* to fear in that moment, it will only be natural then for happiness to appear as a conceptual alternative to fear. If we then gently and non-defensively say, *"No, this is not Being"* to happiness as well (which could be quite counter-intuitive to do at first), our ever creative and reliable self-illusion will produce a third alternative to the second no, such as "Happy, when it comes to X" or a fourth "Fearful, when it comes to Y". If we then again gently and non-defensively say, *"No, this is not Being"* to the third and fourth, and fifth, or sixth, or seventh proposal as well as whatever may come as the eighth, ninth, tenth, eleventh proposal on the part of self-illusion and so on, we will arrive at a point where self-illusion *runs out of options* to solve what it perceives to be a problem. *When self-illusion runs out of options, profound silence manifests and again, subject and object dissolve, leading into the vast space of Curflexion.* This kind of internal silence is an exquisite door into Curflexion because it is not the silence of non-awareness (as when we are deeply asleep), it is not the silence of overwhelming confusion and it is not the silence of repression. It is the silence of all openness and all possibilities. It is Curflexive silence.

The experience of Curflexive silence that derives from this resolution is not a result of mental manipulation, rationalization, effort or interpretation. As stated before, in order for this exploration to yield original silence, we need to have a genuine and experiential understanding of triparadoxia. Our exploration needs to be honest and genuine and not the result of forcing ourselves into a false form or space or silence (which would only produce more noise as we now know).

If we examine our internal experience under the influence of any thought or emotion and gently say, "No, this is not Being" or "This is unsustainable" as well as to its counter proposal, and to its counter, counter proposal and to its counter, counter, counter proposal and so on, and so forth, we will surely eventually arrive to the end of dualization. When we end up saying, "No, this is not Being" or

"This is unsustainable" to "No, this is not Being" or "This is unsustainable", we will be closing the circle of reflexion, where self-illusion will be unable to provide any more options to sustain itself, and *we will then effortlessly fall into our own Curflexive silence.*

Finally, when we experience Curflexive silence as a result of sustained and profound understanding, we will need to additionally let go of any concept around Curflexive silence itself, allowing our experience as the absolute pure embodiment of unobstructed Being to manifest. In this way, silence becomes truly original silence without even the concept of original silence. This allows our consciousness-as-mirror to reflect itself upon itself as a result of complete absence of any form within, deriving in the perfect unobstructed experience of uncontrived inner space.

Yes

It seems to be indeed true that the force that sustains everything also sustains each and every single one of the dual manifestations of self-illusion. While these manifestations are not Being itself, they are surely part of Being. As we recognize each and every one of them, as offered by self-illusion in the form of dualistic proposals and counter proposals, without generating any form of attachment or reactivity to any of these in particular, we allow for Being to manifest through us.

In a similar way to the previous exercise, we can also access boundless space by welcoming everything that manifests in consciousness-as-mirror by gently saying *"Yes, this is part of Being."* In this case, we would also need to *kindly address all subsequent proposals offered on the part of self-illusion with the same welcoming statement until we reach the space of Curflexion.*

For example, if we are experiencing a form of worry in our consciousness-as-mirror, we can welcome worry by saying "Yes, this is part of Being" to which self-illusion will probably respond or add to it by presenting several other sequential counter or subsequent proposals or issues to which we also gently answer saying: "Yes, this is part of Being," until we get to a point where we can see anything and everything that manifests in consciousness-as-mirror as indeed a part of Being, or an aspect of Being without it being Being in and of itself.

It is important to address all proposals and counter-proposals coming from self-illusion until we get to the experience of open space. We will notice that if we stop the process midway we may get stuck in a dualistic proposal and hence we might end up validating it, therefore settling back into the realm of separation. As open space manifests, we should then invite ourselves to breathe deeply and continually as we expand this experience as much as possible without generating any attachment towards it.

One Plus One Is One

When we identify *opposing* thoughts and ideas, we can also bring them together by *dissolving the two into one whole experience of Being*. This is the true all-receiving nature of Being. By doing this, we end up experiencing wholeness as the actual essence of Curflexion, which, as noted before, embodies both opposites of everything that manifests: *all possible dual aspects as one expanded and sustaining whole.*

As we have explored before, self-illusion traditionally and naturally dissects our perception into opposing dualities without this process having any grounding in the reality of Being. In our daily lives, through the direction of self-illusion, we naturally and innocently attempt to attract some elements of Being and, at the same time, generate aversion or rejection towards its opposites or the forces that we perceive pose a threat to what we want. In this way, we experience the essential inner split that is the origin and source of our confusing human condition. In order to address this, we have several options as presented so far in this book. In this instance, as it has been the case for centuries in the Taoist tradition, *we can also say yes to both dualities of a same concept, dissolving two apparently opposing positions into one whole and allow for this new expanded perception of oneness to be fully embodied within.*

In some cases, this pairing can lead to a new duality resulting from the union of the first two. If a new duality manifests, we then add a counter duality to the new duality and we dissolve both of them into a new whole. If there is opposition to that new whole, we add the new opposing duality and so on and so forth, until we reach a state of all-encompassing and non-differentiated space, where we can continuously experience the fullness of Being.

It is important to remind ourselves that at the level of self-illusion, absolutely every thought, emotion, word, sensation and vision (in essence, all expressions of form reflected in our consciousness-as-mirror) are dual. In other words, all can be presented with an opposite to it or a duality of it. If we could imagine a scale where in one extreme we find our most solid expression of self-illusion and at the other side we find Curflexion, we would be able to say that the closer we are to the extreme side of self-illusion, the more solid opposing forces we will experience and perceive in our lives and not only that, but also the more real they will appear to us. On the contrary, the more we situate ourselves towards the side of Curflexion, the less opposing positions we will perceive in our lives and the more unity and harmony we will experience as well as a profound sense of being complete.

As an example of how to practice this particular exercise, at any time, when we notice we are experiencing some form of suffering within, such as sadness for example, we first notice and allow the sadness completely and fully in the canvas of our body, without any bargaining or wanting for it to be solved, changed or end. As we allow sadness completely, we then seek for its opposite duality to manifest at the same time within the canvas of our body, which, in this case, would be happiness. While the notion of sadness lives its own expression freely, we also begin to experience the distinct notion of happiness, *both clearly differentiated, but at the same time,* and as we are doing with sadness, we also welcome happiness completely in the canvas of our body.

As we are able to sustain and feel comfortable with both experiences within, fully allowing and welcoming both dualities, we move a step forward to *allow these two energies to dissolve into an expanded form of energy that contains both fully as they are,* not in conflict, not in turbulence and not as tension, *but as the full experience of Being* that can sustain both forms of energy dissolving into an *expanded* form or energy. In order to do this successfully, it is very important to provide ample space for this new energy formation. *Complete expansion* is the idea that comes to mind at this stage, as far as it needs to go and in all the directions it needs to go, in order to sustain both dualities dissolved into one expanded, inclusive and vast new form of energy. As these two opposites integrate into one, we do not try to define the experience, polarize it, plan it, or modify it. We simply allow and breathe, allow and breathe again, as we relax into this state for as long as comfortably possible.

When we are in a situation where we are not able to clearly identify what we are experiencing initially (as it happens sometimes) or we may not be able to initially label what is going on inside of us clearly as a particular emotion, thought, word, vision or content, we can, at any moment, focus on the canvas of our body without labeling or judging what is going on. We can then completely allow that raw sensation as it is, without labeling it, without wanting it to change. As we do this, and without rejecting it or turning away from it, *we intuitively summon its opposite raw energy* as well to then dissolve and fully integrate both positions into one whole expanded space in the canvas of our body, without eliminating each of the original energies as well, expanding and breathing, until both combine into a stable all-encompassing energy that goes as far as it needs to in any space and direction necessary.

The natural end result of this experience produces profound inner containment, given that, by definition, the union of opposites cannot be described through language or conceptualization when the internal duality has been resolved. In this case, there is no internal quarrel anymore. The duality has been resolved, not by one side attacking the other or winning over the other, but *by the mutual welcoming, dissolution, and embodiment of the opposites into a form of energy that is all-encompassing, all-allowing, expansive, and utterly indescribable.* This is, again, the space of Curflexion, where Being-As-Is is not sectioned into parts, and where we do not feel separated or alienated from the wholeness of Being. This wholeness becomes full presence, full aliveness, full clarity, and full compassion.

As we fully welcome, allow, and unify inner dualities as they manifest within, self-illusion will come to a point where it will run out of options to sustain its quest for separation and will gently give way, having nothing to hold on to, thus allowing full Being to manifest. This process may be very quick or it may require the dissolution of a few rounds of opposites as a new dual experience is formed to then be dissolved and so on and so forth. In any case, when we arrive at the space that contains both positions dissolved as one in gentle and fulfilling Curflexive silence, we relax into it as we breathe deeply to prolong the experience as much as possible.

Origin

In the analogy of Curflexion as a curved reflexion, finding and resting our reflecting consciousness in the same curving mirror may be one of the most powerful realizations we can have. When subject and object disappear and infinite reflection manifests, there is boundless Being available and fully contained at the same time. It is important to remember that rather than understanding the analogy as finding an additional internal mirror to oppose an original mirror (hence, falling into the trap of two), we should understand it more as a curve *from consciousness into consciousness itself.* If we look for something else, then our creative and confusing illusory self will deliver as many renderings of the interpretation of this *other* mirror as it can muster and, again, deliver us into a cyclical dualistic entrapment.

The modality of self-reflection of our consciousness we are looking to experience is a continuum onto itself, where consciousness is never separated from consciousness and is not looking for something else. Rather, it self-reflects from itself unto itself; therefore, it is looking for itself without actually searching for something other than itself. This is not a logical or intuitive process. Being this case, we would then need to come up with a bit of a trick *to get consciousness to see consciousness itself,* given that it is not its natural state at the moment.

Having consciousness-as-mirror perceive pure consciousness-as-mirror is difficult in the same way that an eye cannot see an eye in and of itself and needs a reflective surface to do so, like a mirror, glass, or water. Consciousness cannot *see* itself naturally in the same way it can see form. Actually, our consciousness is used to and is highly skilled in seeking form: be it mental, emotional, or physical. So, how can we have consciousness suddenly look for itself? *Well, by sincerely and honestly seeking something that we firmly believe exists, but it does not actually exist.* In this way, we engage in an honest and sincere search for form through which consciousness ends up staring directly at consciousness, given that there is, in essence, nothing to find.

However, what would that be? What could we search for that we truly believe exists, but that does not actually exist? You may have guessed it. The answer of course would be self-illusion, but how do we actually seek and try to truly find self-illusion? We seek self-illusion first *by noticing self-illusion's apparent activity,* such as thoughts, projections, wants, needs, emotions, or aversions and then by *honestly seeking the actual origin or source of that activity* (Godman, 1989) as practiced in the Advaita tradition of non-dual philosophy.

For example, if I notice myself thinking that I feel anxious, I then seek for the origin of that thought or that emotion, and then I rest and remain in honest, open, internal inquiry and observation in order to genuinely seek for the origin of the thought or emotion. I can also ask myself: "Who thinks the thought I am anxious?" and then rest in open inquiry, while seeking the source of the thought or the emotion. This is an extraordinarily powerful exercise.

We should earnestly look to experience finding the origin of self-illusion or self-illusion in and of itself (Godman, 1989). When we internally seek the origin of a certain thought or emotion, we should honestly allow ourselves to seek openly for the source, without buying into any rationalization or conceptualization. In other words, we seek for self-illusion without answering to our inquiry with another mental form, but rather we seek for the actual origin of self within, in and of itself. We seek for the actual space from where thoughts, emotions, conceptualizations and language emerge or manifest. What we explore is our internal realm and what we are looking for is the concrete origin of who we might be. It can certainly feel strange at first, or a bit contrived, or out of our comfort zone; nevertheless, as we clear that particular experiential path, which may have not been used before, the effect of this exercise can be immediate and extremely powerful.

Inevitably, as we practice and seek for the origin of who we are, we will find through our own direct experience, that there is *actually nothing or no one there*, that there is only space, that there is only all-sustaining silence, and that self-illusion is actually a fabrication and that it has always been a fabrication. In our honest search, we will suddenly find ourselves staring at the seeker itself, and in this way, closing the dualistic *seeker cycle* and reducing it to the primordial union where subject and object resolve and again, Curflexive silence manifests.

This has to be a profoundly experiential process of discovery and deep realization in order for us to embody the transformation that this process will bring. Holding the conceptual thought that self-illusion does not exist, as opposed to experiencing fruitlessly seeking for it internally and experientially *knowing, through self-realization*, that it does not actually exist as a result of this exploration, will result in true liberation, rather than just another conceptual construct getting in the way of our expansion and realization.

In this exercise, we can initially use all kinds of phenomena that are perceived internally. For example, if I suddenly notice that I am cold, I can ask myself, "Who is thinking the thought that I am cold?" or "What is the origin of the thought that I am cold?" or even "Who is actually cold?" If I get an "I am cold" response, then I can inquire, "Who am I" or "Where am I" or "What am I" and remain in honest exploration. As another example, if I suddenly think that something should not have happened, I can ask myself "Who is thinking the thought that something should not have happened?" or "Where or what is the origin of that thought?"

Every element that is reflected and therefore perceived in our consciousness-as-mirror is the perfect material for this exploration. This process is available to us every second of every waking moment, regardless of our previous trespasses, great accumulation of virtue or our endless years of transformational practice. Form as reflected in consciousness-as-mirror is the prime material of our continuous existential exploration and further liberation.

As suggested earlier, we are not seeking an answer in the form of a thought, a word, a concept, or a narrative. We are seeking the direct experience of the actual source of who we might be and for this, we use the natural tendency of self-illusion to seek for an answer to everything, only to, *in a way, trick self-illusion into staring back at the actual search for itself, in this way actualizing Curflexion in that particular instant.* The realization that there is no central self needs to be a lived, experiential phenomenon, in the same way we acquire the lived, experiential realization that water is scarce in the desert by actually seeking for it in deep thirst.

We do not ask who is thinking a particular thought just to respond, "Me, of course" to then end the exploration, further validating and solidifying self-illusion. This is just a concept-driven answer. Rather, we ask what is the origin of a thought to then earnestly and wholeheartedly attempt to locate the source of the thought, or the origin of the thought, or the origin of ourselves.

Intellectually, we may now know that our internal exploration to locate a central self will come back as unsuccessful. We are not seeking an answer to the question; rather, *we are seeking the actual resulting experience of space in which, through seeking self, we actually realize that it is non-existent.* If we do not actually and honestly engage in that exploration, we will continually fall back into the abstract dualistic narrative and descriptive models in which we currently base our experience of self.

There will be absolutely no doubt in your core when you reach the Curflexive state. You will know without a doubt when you get to the point where you actually know that there is no one in there, as you experience your consciousness-as-mirror reflected as reflexion of itself. When this happens, we may get suddenly startled and the experience may not last long. With acclimatization, these periods will be longer and longer. My best advice at this point is to call on your breath when you get there and expand what we feel to be our energy field as a way to encompass the vastness of the experience. In other words, as soon as we notice we are there, that we are a part of the infinite space of Being, we can then breathe and expand whatever we perceive to be our energy or presence in that space without limit, while breathing and expanding again towards infinite space. If necessary, we can symbolically expand this sensation of vastness to all the corners of all the limitless universes in all the realms of all possibilities.

In my experience, it only requires one good, honest look into the nature of self-illusion to initially see the delusion for ourselves: the space behind the daily internal quarrel. Once we have made that honest trip once, or a few of times, the path could be always there. After this, it is just a matter of *deepening and expanding the experience to the point where space is completely evident and there is absolutely no doubt in our mind that self-illusion is a fabrication;* when we reach this point, the illusory construction of self-illusion resolves entirely.

It is important to remind ourselves again at this point that, like all other approximations to Curflexion, this is not a cumulative experience that will lead to a goal or another experience or understanding that will lead to another goal. It may seem sequential, in that the experience deepens as a result of continuing visits into the space of Curflexion. The destination is exactly the same every single time we seek for the origin of our thoughts and emotions. The only difference we will see is that we will be able to remain in Curflexion for longer and more stable periods of time. Furthermore, we will also notice that the more we remain in that space, the more we will be able to experience Being in all its radiance, if we must use words to describe it.

The experience of Being is a natural and uncaused manifestation of the absence of noise and internal debris, rather than something we have attained, built, arranged for, or constructed. Our engagement in this experience needs to be free of hope or gain, free of any accumulation, and free of merit, addition, or particular expectations. What we are looking for (without looking for it) is the space that remains after we have dissolved looking for a central self. As self-illusion resolves, light is allowed to shine through the Curflexive condition of our consciousness seeking itself. This is not light that we have created, achieved, or manifested as a result of our dedication, effort, or sacrifice. This is light that has always been there, all along and throughout all our struggles. We were just not able to notice it anymore, or it could not get to us through all the conceptual clutter. So the actual struggle, tension, and strategy invested in attempting to create the light of Being within ourselves was precisely, and ironically, what actually blocked us from seeing that same light.

Liberating Language

Poetry has the seemingly magical power of dissolving the rigidity of language and polarization. When used in particular ways, it has the power of opening the door to Curflexion. Poetry has been historically and consistently used in environments where individuals have successfully managed to resolve their self-illusion. I am not necessarily talking about the rigid kind of poetry that comes with metrics and rules, given that these structures may interfere with the deconstruction of language itself and, therefore, eliminate its potential for transformation.

I call it Liberating Language, using language with absolute freedom and flexibility to allow for the constant deconstruction and liberation of dualization, while providing endless attempts to lure self-illusion so as to describe the indescribable and then to resolve into unsustainable space. This use of language allows self-illusion to trust some form of potential accomplishment, grounding or settling, some form of validation or understanding to then al-

197

low for pristine open space to completely engulf our experience.

Liberating Language allows for the precious dance of triparadoxia to fill up all corners of self-illusion to then elegantly deliver its own resolution. An experience of resolution that leaves no room for argument, that allows no re-interpretation, categorization, or re-evaluation; one that dawns profound certainty of our triparadoxial condition, therefore leaving no doubt of its certainty and allowing for profound peace and clarity as a result of fully resting in Being.

To engage in the production of Liberating Language, we do not need to be highly literate; we do not need to be language majors or even know how to read and write. We would just need a basic understanding of triparadoxia to start playing a game that resolves self-illusion: the game of reaching complete and irreversible Curflexive silence, the game that delivers the everlasting presence of full absence of polarized form.

Liberating Language has many ways of being approximated. An option could be to build the edifice of certainty only to then eliminate all solid grounding for that initial platform. This allows for language and dualization to lose their sustainment and form. It also allows for endless attempts to describe the indescribable, to gently or powerfully soften the notion of a solid, consistent and rigid reality.

Liberating Language can easily, poignantly and elegantly illustrate the absurdity of seeking attainment, only to lose everything in the end. At the same time, it also allows for inspiring and powerful descriptions of the absence of any solid platform for self-illusion. Liberating Language also has the ability of speaking in the closest form possible to Being, the kind of language that has no worry of further validation.

To practice Liberating Language, we just need a pen and paper, or a good friend to take notes, or simply our speech or internal dialogue, for us to then invoke the adventure of resolving each polarized moment. We can express Liberating Language whenever we find it viable to do so. There are many approaches to engage in Liberating Language, and each of us can find our own style.

First, for example, we could start by noticing and expressing the solid form or condition that is currently in front of us, or we can initiate with an expression that would enhance or sustain self-illusion. Secondly, we can problematize or scrutinize the condition inspired by the three paradoxes. Then on a third and last stage, we may allow for all the build-up of the initial problematic condition and the following triparadoxial attenuation to resolve the edifice of the initial proposal. It could be something like this:

Thoughts colluding in the center,
granting confusion its daily plea.
Living the internal entrapment
built by our own innocence.

Lured by the flashing lights of certainty,
and the understanding of our profound complaint,
we seek to build a world of polarities
out of pure breath.

A heart of gold will never be created
in the shining castle of the known
for it will only attain bliss
in the extent that it is gone!

As we understand these three stages, we can then make them longer, shorter, interchangeable, and reversible. We can change the order, the intensity, the complexity and the uniqueness of the language being used so that we may speak evermore directly to self-illusion and gently guide it into its own resolution through the embrace of Being. You can find examples of Liberating Language in the appendix of this book.

It is always good practice to keep our own writing available to review when we feel we need to. Our expression of this kind of language ends up becoming reliable paths into Curflexion, paths that are unique to ourselves, that are relevant to our particular context and experience, paths that create louder and more profound resonance towards our own complete liberation.

These paths are particularly effective because they are made to suit. No other prayer, no other song and no other form of poetry regardless of its author will speak to you louder, more powerfully, and more directly than your own. The reason for this is, as has been said before, that your individual door into Curflexion is as absolutely unique as your fingerprints, and this is why the way must be fully travelled on our own. No other code, no other set of guidelines, expectations, or axioms will suit you as your own.

When we create paths into the state of Curflexion through Liberating Language, we explore our own internal landscape, and we clear the path inwards towards the infinite center without a center, to the brightest light possible without any actual light, and to the eternal song without any actual melody.

Inquiry-Based Coaching™ (IBC)

As a result of many years of sharing and practice, we have developed our own model of inquiry at the Innerland Institute (innerland.com). We call this method **Inquiry-Based Coaching™**. IBC is an extraordinarily powerful methodology that we use to help our clients access the curflexive space in order to identify and transform transcendental perceptional obstacles into clear and actionable life opportunities.

We have shared this method with hundreds of people, dozens of teams, and several organizations so far with extraordinary results. Through IBC, we first support our clients in identifying the most pressing hindrances to their lives. Then, we present them with a series of questions and exercises where they deeply experience what gets in the way of their passion, purpose and success. We then guide them through a process in which they access their own inner curflexive space, being able to then create extraordinary

203

outcomes that often they had not even imagined. We finally invite our clients to take responsibility and apply these deep, fresh, and new realizations in their lives, accompanied by the incredible clarity, connection, and empowerment that result from the application of this method. IBC can be practiced in the form of self-facilitation or as a guided process with the support of someone else. In essence, this method uses our current manifesting life situations as well as past pains, and future fears, to deeply and existentially realize what is needed, how is it needed, and when.

IBC has five phases. *First*, we clearly identify the issue at hand. This is a very important step in the process. Given that we take for granted much of our inner noise, allowing ourselves to notice and realize our hindrances as such is paramount to the process. Many of us have adopted an "ALL OK" mindset to be able to survive our lives, when in reality the winds of confusion and doubt are blowing full force inside us. *Second*, after clearly identifying a perceptional obstacle that is getting in the way of our expansion and freedom, we wholly explore it so as to deeply appreciate how it shows up for us internally and externally. In this phase, we also are able to see the depth and complexity of its manifestation. *Third*, we explore the impact that our own validation and holding of this perception actually has in our lives. What manifests from validating this hindrance? How do I separate or abandon myself? How do I freeze, overreact, or run away? Who do I "turn into" in my mind when I validate the obstacle as real and impenetrable? *Fourth*, through accessing the curflexive space of inner clarity and understanding, we invite ourselves to see and experience our lives beyond or without validating our own self-created experience of constriction, giving birth to new, clear, and fresh insights that are relevant, real, and actionable. *Fifth*: action. What is next? How? When? With whom? What are the clear, evident, natural, next steps for you after realizing all of the above? Follow-through and commitment both naturally and effortlessly arise filling our lives with purpose, understanding, and deep realization.

The results of the application of this methodology in executive and life coaching environments, as well as in organizations so far have been truly extraordinary. Our data shows a clear increase of more than 50% average after one year of practice in major personal and leadership attributes such as enthusiasm, clarity, commitment, flexibility, courage, openness, receptivity, patience, trust, presence, responsibility, and equanimity amongst others.

At the Innerland Institute we also currently offer an accreditation program to become an **IBC Coach**™. This program will prepare you to deeply practice and integrate the methodology in order to be able to share it with individuals or organizations all around the world. Our graduates go through a truly life changing experience that enables them to further share it with others. Learn more of our programs, events, and sessions at **innerland.com**

7
Sustainment

I have been found and lost
O, so many times!
When does it end?
Where is such sight?

I have travelled the path
O, each time anew.
Never the same signs
singing the same plight!

O, I have seen the treasure!
and became distracted
by the old songs of
the old world.

When will it end?
It will end when we un-yarn
only this last thread.

Breath

Once we are able to experience Curflexion, to abide in the space where there is no intermediary, the walls of confusion and conditioning begin to dissolve. We begin to experience a new space within, a space of fulfilling silence, a space of direct non-dual experience, a space of grounding, a space of action, a space of excitement, engagement and sustainment, regardless of whatever is manifesting in our life. Having been feeding self-illusion for so long, this process will need our sustained attention for some time in order for us to be able to completely eliminate all traces of attachment to form from our inner experience.

We should not expect thoughts to disappear from our experience. As much as these practices may allow for situations where we could actually be completely free of internal form for good periods of time, stopping the natural generation or emanation of thoughts altogether would be as improbable as the cessation of cloud formations in the sky. Thoughts will continue to manifest consistently even as we become fully immersed in Being-As-Is. What is different however, is how we will now interact with inner form and what thoughts now experientially mean to us.

When we talk about space and silence in the realm of Being, we should not think of a barren void of darkness, but rather of Curflexive silence, a profound experience sustained by a complete embodiment of space and peace in the midst of form, action and interaction. A form of playful, compassionate, grounded and committed dance with thoughts where we deeply know that we actually are an indivisible component of the infinite space that sustains all expressions of internal form, rather than being the particular expressions of form themselves.

Once we are familiar with this space for some time, as we come in and out of the Curflexive experience, as we notice and then lose the experience and then gain the experience again, it is important to allow for Curflexion to gently and naturally prolong as much as possible, without falling into the traps of want, fix, attachment or gain, welcoming and surrendering to the experience of letting go.

In order to prolong the experience of Curflexion, *we can use our breath to anchor ourselves to the presence of the space within.* When we notice that there is no inherent origin of our internal experience, that there is no inherent source of content to our internal experience and therefore, that true experience is actually empty of any solid form, weight or implication, we suddenly find ourselves in a space that cannot be described, communicated, or contextualized. In order to prolong this experience of space and grounding without generating internal discourse or attachment, *we can anchor ourselves into our breath, in order to gently allow for the space to continue, in order for us to naturally surrender into the realm of eternal possibilities.* As we breathe, we keep noticing the space inside, noticing the stability of Being-as-Is, noticing the vastness of the continually present movements, sounds, and conditions all around us without interpreting, buying into, expecting, or requiring anything.

It is important to know that placing our attention on our breath as a way into Curflexion will usually not work if you are not already there. When we attempt to seek Curflexion through focusing on or following our breath, we are establishing a methodology seeking results, attempting to control, to monitor, to evaluate and to assess the process, and therefore, we will fall again, without noticing, into the 2-for-1 Paradox.

When we seek, want, strategize, or cajole for an experience in this way, we necessarily begin to evaluate what we are doing and may begin asking ourselves questions such as: "Is this experience it?" "Is that it?" "Am I there now?" "How long will it take?" "Is there something else more reliable?" "How does it actually feel?" "Ah, maybe THIS is it?" and so on, generating considerable noise and falling back into the space of self-illusion. So, when we engage in this dualistic process of want, achievement, and evaluation, we are actually removing ourselves from unconditional surrender. We lose the experience, as we are actually seeking something other than what we have in this instant.

Breath is a stabilizer for Curflexion and not a door into Curflexion. By allowing breath to stabilize our non-dual experience once we are there, we prolong the space within to a point where even the concepts of welcoming, allowing and surrender dissolve into the ever-present space of full inclusion.

Shortcuts

As we further allow the experience of Curflexion to deepen and stabilize, it is important to remind ourselves that regardless of the method, process or sequence we follow, this is all in all a deconstructive process rather than a constructive one. The experience of Curflexion deepens *as we allow, surrender, and welcome, rather than as we fix, add, or transform.* It is about resting in Being rather than building and it is about noticing rather than visualizing or projecting.

Allowing ourselves to resolve self-illusion is, in essence, the entire quest: the ultimate internal travel. For some time, especially at the beginning of our exploration into Curflexion, this quest may seem confusing, at times overwhelming, and at times may even seem impossible. The assurance of the Curflexive experience will deepen and become undeniable as we notice and discover for ourselves what is actually self-evident behind self-illusion.

As we access Curflexion and then lose the same state of Curflexion for some time while we are not able to permanently rest in the experience, we could certainly notice some non-causal approaches that may work for us particularly well in order to allow Curflexion back into our lives in a fast and efficient way.

We may need different approaches to access the non-dual state. It is very important at this point to consider our own guidance to be of utmost importance. If we are using a particular approach that seems not to be working, most probably, it actually is not. *At all times and in all situations, as we practice and allow for Curflexion, we remain fully responsible for our understanding, for our experience and for our actions.* So, if a particular approach it is not working, simply move on. You and only you would know what is working or not, because you and only you can experience Curflexion for yourself.

Stabilizing Curflexion is a process that is not intended to take our entire life, or several lifetimes or several eons, or whatever extended timeframe we would like to use. Rather, depending on the intensity of our allowing of Being, it could only take a short period of time. To do so, we need to repeatedly allow for the path inwards to the space behind/before all the form and noise, and as we notice effective approaches to it, we could take note of them and consider them to be shortcuts into the infinite space of Being. Shortcuts could be sentences, words, sounds or particular practices that are truly powerful and effective in taking us directly into Being.

These shortcuts are our very own and come from the depths of Curflexion. When we are immersed in the non-dual space, we suddenly experience realizations of such clarity that are often impossible to fully describe, but which may be easily identified with a sound, a word or a short question or phrase. When we abide in Curflexion and we notice we are immersed in this state, a sound may manifest from within, a word may manifest, a question may manifest, a phrase or an image may manifest creating a strong association with the state we are experiencing. These are shortcuts to Curflexion, and the more we use them, the more we identify them and the more they resonate with our profound internal experience of freedom, the more powerful they become.

After we identify them, though, there is a risk of over-using them to the point where they lose their effectiveness or we risk demanding too much out of them, or we may end up using them to try to fix an unpleasant state of mind, which will only make the situation more complicated delivering us back into confusion. The other risk is mistaking the sound, word, phrase or question with the actual Curflexive experience itself. In these cases, shortcuts will not work as expected. It is crucial to remember that self-illusion can use absolutely anything that appears in consciousness-as-mirror as an object of distraction, as an object of comparison, judgment, polarization, evaluation, separation or as a settling platform for self-illusion. Easily and often unnoticed, our shortcuts could become the illusion itself. So, it is important to keep them fresh and sincerely rooted in the clear understanding of the three paradoxes.

As we experience Being-As-Is and are able to rest in the center without a center, the space that sustains and allows everything, these shortcuts will naturally manifest. In other cases, we may read a shortcut from someone else as we abide in a Curflexive space and adopt it because it strongly resonates to a point where it now becomes ours based on our path and experience.

Variety

It is easy to see that self-illusion is extraordinarily nimble. It is precisely this quality that allows it to sometimes come in through our perceptional back door to regain the space of our awareness moving us back into the dualistic experience. Because of this, we should know that it is highly improbable that only one of these practices or any single practice in particular should always work in a consistent and reliable way. This is the reason why I have included several practices in the previous section that offer different approximations into the same space. We need to be aware that self-illusion might probably develop a form of resistance to any particular practice we use for a while. This is the reason why we may want to continuously vary the practices available to us.

We may find that a particular practice or approach is working very well for some time or for some times in our day or even for some weeks or months. Sooner or later, it may not work anymore as self-illusion might have rooted itself within the same exercise somehow without our noticing, and is now using that particular approach to solidify its illusory identity to attempt to achieve, fix, arrange, modify, or polarize our experience. How do we know that the illusion has taken over? Because at this point the results of our actions tend to backfire and our experience seems heavy, dualized, complicated, frustrating or confusing, rather than spacious and liberating.

If we get caught trying to fix our internal condition in any way, or trying to achieve something as a product of using these practices or if we notice that we are now tensely expecting liberation to arrive, or wondering whether it has actually arrived, or how long will it take, or how well we are doing, then we are back into the space of polarization. When we notice this, we can simply, gently, and kindly welcome self-illusion with another allowing approach suggested in the previous practices, or we can simply welcome and ground self-illusion in the canvas of our body.

It is very important to remind ourselves not to objectify or personify self-illusion in any way. In essence, self-illusion is clearly not something or someone in particular. Again, this is actually the point of the illusion. Rather, self-illusion should be understood simply as a mirage, as a *perceptional illusion* in the same way we experience *optical illusions*. Therefore, as self-illusion resolves, we actually do not loose anything while at the same time we become fully alive, grounded and complete. It is also important at this point to notice and acknowledge that these Curflexive practices are still using a basic form of structurally dualistic elements (including language and polarization) for the purposes of engaging and eventually resolving the illusory self, thus generating and presenting interesting situations.

As our practice moves along, we can review which one of these practices is working better by noticing where our perception is at the time. As time goes by and with practice, it will be very easy for us to notice if what we are using as a practice at any given time *is allowing us more space or it is taking us into a situation where there is less space and is more contrived.* We will be able to clearly feel this in our body, in our emotions and in the type of thoughts we are having, regardless of where we are or the apparent conditions surrounding us at any given time.

The signs of confusion happening are that we notice ourselves getting caught up in our thoughts and emotions. We tend to see them as real, relevant, polarized, valid and in need of attention. We also notice that these forms start demanding our energy and time in cyclical ways, resulting in our cyclically addressing the same worries or concerns or some form of derivation or modification of these, and then moving onto others. In terms of our emotions, we would also begin to experience worry, stress, fear, anticipation, or anxiety.

As time goes by and with direct experience of this process, you will be able to design or modify your own approximations and practices to access Curflexion. We all have experienced unique and different events and situations that are particular to our lives, and some of these may serve as unique frames of reference to access the exquisite space of all possibilities.

We can practice accessing Curflexion in countless situations. The only tools we need in order to be able to access Curflexion are (a) daily life, (b) our consciousness-as-mirror, (c) the basic understanding of triparadoxia, and (d) the initial exercises into the nature of our reality described in the previous section while you develop your own. This would be our only travel pack into the infinite space of Being.

Depth

As stated before in the book, it is clear that all these practices can be engaged in at any time without the need of any procedural, sequential, formal or structural methodology. There is no need to change our names, renounce the comforts of modern life or seclude ourselves in permanent retreat. Nevertheless, there is one element to these practices that will yield extraordinary results when applied in a consistent way: *depth*.

Depth speeds the process of resolution of self-illusion substantially. If we make a point of engaging in any of the practices suggested in this book (or any of your own) in a deep, consistent and purposeful manner, our understanding of triparadoxia will permeate our lives profoundly and will generate extraordinary outcomes.

Depth can be created in several ways. Depth emerges as a result of profound personal experience with the source or object of our inquiry. We deeply experience something when we *give it all our attention* and when we are *fully committed to freely embodying it*, to making it ours, to consume it or to fuse with it, yet without grasp, without demand and without expecting any particular outcome in return. If we take some time off from time to time to focus in our internal process, the deeper and more profound our understanding and transformation will be. Taking time off without having to substantially alter our busy lives to fully engage in the deep experience of the profound assimilation of triparadoxia can be the cornerstone of our final, complete, and irreversible embodiment of Curflexion.

As we initially naturally alternate coming in and out between dual and non-dual states of consciousness when we begin our Curflexive exploration, it is important to know that the deeper we go, the shorter the oscillation we will live between both experiences. The more profound and prolonged our incursions into the non-dual state, the more understanding and therefore the deeper our resolution of the illusory self.

Depth can be accessed in several ways. We do not need a prescribed setting or a particular procedure. However we frame it, there is only one thing to consider above all when it comes to this aspect: *depth simply requires all our attention.* However we engage with creating depth, it is up to us, depending on our preferences and personalities, as to how this should look like in particular. In essence, distractions need to be put aside. We have many options; we can be sitting comfortably or lying down, closing our eyes, or fixing them on an object, letting go of distractions and focusing our attention internally as deeply as we can.

There is no prescribed time allotted to doing this as well. We can give ourselves anything from a few minutes to even hours per day, or several days even, to fully look inwardly into our Curflexive universe, while we allow for our full attention to connect with the absence of form, as well as the space behind the noise, so that we may be able to engage in the practices we have discussed previously or the ones of your own creation.

As a suggestion, I have included the following:

Depth Exercise

1. Sit or lie comfortably.
2. Rest, relax, and breathe deeply.
3. Draw your attention to your inner space and see what is naturally manifesting internally in the present moment. You can work with anything that is presently there, including fear, stress, apprehension, panic, paranoia, anxiety, confusion, tension, dread, excitement, anticipation, elation, happiness, expectation, hope, illusion, desire, or even neutral form.
4. Absolutely welcome what is manifesting, allowing and supporting it to live its life fully and completely as a thought, emotion, or sensation in the canvas of your body, without buying into it, acting on it, and at the same time, without expecting anything to be different

than it is and without expecting any particular results from it.

5. Allow, surrender, welcome, breathe, and expand your energy. Allow, surrender, welcome, breathe, and expand your energy again and again. Allow, surrender, welcome, breathe, and expand your energy, profusely throughout the exercise.

6. After a while, and depending on your internal circumstance, you can additionally use the following methods to address any situation in your consciousness-as-mirror: *Triparadoxia, No Option, Yes, One Plus One Is One,* and *Origin,*

7. After a while, and as you are able, abide for as long as possible in the all-spacious realm beyond language, polarization, dualization and form that should naturally remain as a result of these practices, breathing deeply and expanding your energy throughout the exercise.

It is important to remember that if you engage in this practice with the expectation to achieve any kind of results, it will backfire and it will transform into a dualistic-promoting exercise.

The deeper and the more often you engage in this exercise without expecting anything from it, the better and faster results you will have, leading to the eventual and irreversible resolution of the illusory self and, with it, an inalienable welcoming into the expansive and extraordinary space of Curflexion. Depth will generate a strong anchor that will allow you to sustain your Curflexive experience more and more. It will further allow you to come back in a faster and easier way. It will deepen your trust in triparadoxia, and it will allow for you to freely abide in the boundless state of unobstructed understanding and bliss.

Living the Infinite Space

It is clear that we need some kind of support to move from dualism into Curflexion. Dualism does not resolve in and of itself into ever-present and boundless space. We just need to look around or read about the history of humanity. Dualism seems to be self-perpetuating, and it also seems to have the ability to present countless illusory exit doors that open up into the same space that we are trying to vacate, in an endless cycle of hope, loss, fear, happiness, frustration, elation or forgetfulness.

Dualism gets resolved through the deep existential understanding that language, polarization, and internal structures are only partial expressions of the true manifestation of Being, and that they need to be let go of as solid in order not to get in the way of the original clarity behind all the noise. Also, dualism gets resolved without any effort and by its own accord through the deep existential understanding that our endless cycles of conceptual proposals and counter proposals to fix our internal condition will only end up solidifying our condition and, therefore, our suffering. Finally, given that there is no actual central self, there is nowhere to internally settle, no one to be, no one to become, nothing to achieve and nothing for which to hope. We are absolutely complete here and now – in whatever way we are manifesting.

The form of support needed to move from dualism to Curflexion needs to be swift and efficient, yet completely disposable. It should only take us so far as to the point where we can embody self-reflection, and then we should just kindly and gently jump into all-sustaining space in order to experience Being directly. Interestingly enough, again, there is no need to do anything, fix anything, accumulate anything, discover anything, access a secret or win anything as well. *There is just understanding and allowing.*

In essence, there is actually no jumping, no going and no coming. The resolving happens of its own accord, as we remain noticing and allowing triparadoxia and the resulting space that comes with it, while we let go and surrender into all-sustaining space as a result of the profound understanding of our confusing, cyclical and solidifying condition.

All polarization will naturally resolve or evaporate without leaving any residue behind. As incredible as it may seem, there was nothing there in the first place, resulting in nothing as residue. Sometimes, this resolution will happen slowly or maybe even seem unnoticed. Sometimes, the burning up will happen abruptly, regardless of whether we expect it or not, or whether we want it or not, or whether we even like it or not. In any case, once we are able to sub-stantially puncture the structural framework of polarized illusion, our complete experience of Being will gently manifest through understanding.

In this process, each of us should seek our own pace. Rushing could produce unnecessary suffering, confu-sion, blame, or the settling of self-illusion in an unsustaina-ble platform. At the same time, it is also important to know that it is always viable to rebuild self-illusion. This happens easily when we lose our understanding of triparadoxia and go back into the stream of distraction and confusion. We can always go back to the familiar discomfort of dualistic life, reinstating ourselves as instruments of resistance and want. The experience of a contrived life is never far away and always accessible if we want it. Most of us know this quite well.

If we are willing to allow for the manifestation of the ultimate and primordial expression of who we are, in the end, we need to let go of everything that is not this same primordial expression. There cannot be any hold back or secret space remaining where subject and object quietly sustain their illusory creation. All practices presented in this book are still only signposts to the direct experience of Being, yet apparently needed while we are still a part of the mirage. These approaches to understanding take us all the way to the edge, but once in the edge, we need to allow for the ultimate letting go into everlasting, compassionate, un-obstructed and fully supportive Curflexive space by releasing the approximations that took us there in the first place. All is surrendered as we enter the infinite space of Being in order to sustain the inexpressible perfection of its all-welcoming embrace.

The all-allowing and all-providing sphere is neither inside nor outside, it neither allows or provides anything as well, yet it cannot be doubted given that it becomes self-evident. This sphere is self-sustaining because it is not a concept to be built, it is not a position to be defended, it is not a request to be acquiesced to and it is not an imposition; instead, it is a realization of profound understanding. It would seem that Curflexion might truly be an exquisite and worthwhile experience for humans. *This is simply because all other objectives, every single one of them, will seem to eventually end up polarizing themselves leading to suffering and contraction.*

The experiential exploration of triparadoxia is an extraordinary vessel to allow for liberation to manifest, not because it gives us anything or provides us with some sort of unique or secret understanding. It is precisely the opposite, because it frees us and liberates us through opening all doors, all windows, all nooks and crannies, all rooms, all corridors and passages; and all kinds of attics to the winds of understanding. This would naturally and effortlessly allow for letting go, surrendering, and welcoming the absolute, innate, immediate and un-tarnishable perfection of Being-As-Is. The internal experience of unity and completeness cannot actually be amassed or solidly pointed to in any way. It is simply allowed, as it lives within and cannot be directly expressed or described because it doesn't actually exist, as we understand existence to manifest, yet, ironically, its undeniable presence solves our personal human condition.

As we allow for the direct, clear, and unobstructed light of Curflexion, we finally embark on the quest to surrender to the most pristine and extraordinary expression of who we are beyond all polarization. This is the beginning of life unobstructed, of sense unopposed, of immanent completion, of Curflexive silence containing all action and all meaning, of understanding, of compassion, of peace embodying all possible answers and of contentment, holding, embracing, and loving all possible outcomes. It is the gift of unopposed Being; of complete and undivided experience piercing through every breath, every word, every thought and every concept ever conceived or conceivable. It is the ultimate willingness and the ultimate welcoming of unobstructed freedom.

www.curflexion.com

Appendix:
Liberating Language

Now

Now lives within.
It is the answer behind the answer.
The lost tradition of inquiry.
The clarity that bears everything!

It produces compassion,
yet compassion does not produce it.

It produces bliss,
yet bliss will not take you there.

It gifts you invincibility,
yet invincibility will deceive you.

It manifests peace,
yet peace will not create it.

O, Inner Truth!
Defending nothing,
losing everything.
It is complete.

Emergence

Seekers go into caves,
not because they want to find Truth,
but because they have found it!

They find the lowest places,
not because they want gain,
but because they have already lost everything.

They speak to others,
not because they want something,
but because they already gave up completely.

The spark that burns the fallacy
precedes all liberated action,
and liberated action produces nothing!

O, great whisper!
Uncaused song.
The dream is to be found
where it was never born.

Burn the nightmare while
in the field of the known.
Become the cold waters
and evaporate in the dawn.

Free Will

O amusement.
Master of all!
Why the suffering?
Why the fall?

The empty promise sets ablaze
complete emptiness in our gaze.

Reality dawns consciousness!
We act before we know we want to.
What drives the spell?

River

All phenomena flow into
the river of benediction.

The unavoidable are the perfect
song to go further into empty space.

The avoidable are the playground
of the enlightened fool!

All accounted for.
There is no shore.

The Edge

O so daunting!
Desolation, search, breath, loss.
Quivering dancers,
what do we seek?
The unfathomable!

We walk the edge,
for a glimpse, for a sign,
tormentously, blind.

Wanting with every cell for the spark
that consumes everything.

The Unsaid

All words will end
burnt into the unsaid.
Air, wheezing, grunt.
No meaning but song.

Falling apart,
breath and breeze,
flame and dance,
all there is!

Release what ends it all!
Place it square in my soul.
For only then, I will clearly see,
that there is no one in me.

Sweet Condition

It is the wanting for what others
should want that confines us.

It is defending duality that locks
us in the depths of loneliness.

It is the expectation of bliss
that produces loss.

O, sweet condition!

Destitute of all mental possessions,
the remaining space
sustains everything!

High Ground

I look for you desperately!
O, Shaming High Ground.
Forsaken me now?

I still tremble in anticipation.
Climbing your golden ladder,
heeling to pounce on self-pity,
to savor the flavor of want.

Not there.
No taste.
No hold.
No more.

Clarity

O, elusive whisper!
Capricious song!

I long for you to be within.
I am your beggar and slave.

O condition.
Bright or stale,
when I fail to see
that I am just Space.

Resolution

It is indeed true –
that the measure of all things
is non-existent.

It falsely abides in confusion
within our innocent mind,
self-perpetuating,
and all prevailing.

Language attempts to confine it.
Thought attempts to replace it.

Inspiration is absence.
What is left from complete void,
eternally silent and
perfectly spontaneous.

Great Jewel

Never outside.
Always within.
Dormant.

Slow awakening.
Unhurried song.
Revived.

Self-directing fire
seeking the source.
Empty.

Dropping into space,
loosing oneself.
Everlasting.

Nowhere to go!
Completely fulfilled.
Now.

Payment

When we buy into happiness
we pay with sorrow.

When we buy into hope
we pay with loss.

When we buy into security
we pay with risk.

When we buy into stability
we pay with uncertainty,

When we buy into enlightenment
we pay with doom.

Letting go of both light and darkness
is the only way.

The Fountain

Where is the fountain?
Where is the source of endless gold?
Where is Your Home?

Was it in what was?
Will it be in what will be?
Or is it in the tension
between the two?

Masterful trap!
Endless doors show all the signs.
Every promise ever made,
dancing in delight.

No door!
There is no door!
There never was.
Only rumors and confusion.

Entering the House is letting go
the search for the door.

Just Noise

Just noise.
Only stuttering air
appearing to mean something.

Just language.
Only gamified structure
trying to resemble Being.

Just will.
Only a byproduct of confusion,
summoning the many inner voices.

Just thought.
Only interpreted neutral form
absent of any meaning.

Just emotion.
Only misunderstood life energy
without hope or loss.

Just Being.
Open,
Pristine.

Complete

Majestic!
Splendorous!
It's not this,
but the quiet.

It's how every leaf, spike, and flake
completely surrender to their
exquisite and perfect place.

Nothing out of order.
Absolutely nothing out of order!
In this unnamable silence, everything rests.

Pain is no more.
Hope is no more.
Dread is no more.
All are one and nothing at all.

Everything, simply, rests
as it is
complete.

Done

I'm done.

Even this breath is not mine anymore.
The songs seem to echo,
o, so far away.

What's next?

www.curflexion.com

References

Burton, Neel (2010). *The Art of Failure: The Anti Self-Help Guide. Oxford: Acheron Press.*

Dowman, Keith (2013). Original Perfection: Vairotsana's Five Early Transmissions. *Boston: Wisdom Publications.*

Godman, David (1989). Be As You Are: The Teachings of Sri Ramana Maharshi. *London: Penguin Books.*

Harris, Sam (2012). Free Will. *New York: Free Press.*

Hayes, Steven (2005). Get Out of Your Mind and Into Your Life: The New Acceptance and Commitment Therapy. *Oakland: New Harbinger.*

Hood, Bruce (2012). The Self Illusion: Why There Is No 'You' Inside Your Head. *New York: Harper Perennial.*

38915393R00157